RECOLLECTIONS OF REAGAN

Also by Peter Hannaford

My Heart Goes Home: A Hudson Valley Memoir (editor)
Remembering Reagan (coauthor)
Talking Back to the Media
The Reagans: A Political Portrait

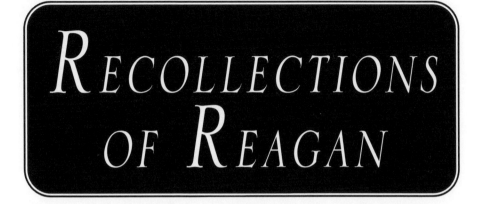

RECOLLECTIONS OF REAGAN

A PORTRAIT OF RONALD REAGAN

Edited by
Peter Hannaford

WILLIAM MORROW AND COMPANY, INC.

NEW YORK

Library of Congress Cataloging-in-Publication Data

Recollections of Reagan : a portrait of Ronald Reagan / edited
  by Peter Hannaford.—1st ed.
      p.   cm.
   ISBN 0-688-14613-9
   1. Reagan, Ronald.   2. Presidents—United States—Biography.
   3. United States—Politics and government—1981-1989.
   I. Hannaford, Peter.
   E877.R43   1997
   973.927'092—dc21
   [B]   97-19129
                                                                          CIP

Printed in the United States of America

First Edition

1   2   3   4   5   6   7   8   9   10

BOOK DESIGN BY BERNARD KLEIN

Dedicated to Ronald Reagan . . .
one of a kind

PREFACE

"What a nice man. It's too bad he can't get elected." That was my first thought as Ronald Reagan disappeared from view after our first meeting, a chance one. It was February 1965, in San Francisco, at the annual midwinter meeting of the California Republican State Central Committee. That Saturday morning, two friends and I had come to help our local assemblyman find out if there was any support for his running for lieutenant governor the next year. We were early, so decided to kill time looking at the commercial exhibits on the mezzanine of the Hilton Hotel. Soon, we saw Ronald Reagan striding toward us down the aisleway, with a couple of aides in tow. He was in the early stages of his exploratory travels around the state to decide whether to become a candidate for governor in 1966. He stopped and chatted with us and we were impressed, but had already decided that the only way to prevent Governor "Pat" Brown from winning a third term was to support San Francisco Mayor George Christopher, a seasoned politician. My friends and I thus joined the army of those who underestimated Ronald Reagan—an army that was to grow much larger in the years ahead.

He not only defeated Christopher in a clean, hard-fought primary, but also went on to swamp Pat Brown, becoming California's thirty-third governor. I was happy to have seen the light, so to speak, in time to vote for him in November that year. One of my friends from that first encounter soon joined the new Reagan administration, as did a number of other friends. On their visits back from Sacramento, they spoke enthusiastically about what was being accomplished by this actor-turned-politician.

In 1971, Governor Reagan appointed me vice chairman of his Consumer Fraud Task Force. Its membership was racially, ethnically, and politically diverse. I was impressed that the only instruction we received from the Governor's Office was that we were to examine areas of consumer fraud and make recommendations. We did, traveling up and down the state. Our job was done when we submitted our report and recommendations to the governor in May 1973.

Not long thereafter, Ned Hutchinson, the governor's appointments secretary, called and asked, "How would you like to be the governor's appointee to the Tahoe Regional Planning Agency?" That was the bistate (California and Nevada) agency created by Congress to oversee development of the rugged-looking, but ecologically fragile, Lake Tahoe Basin. I had long been interested in conservation and said I'd be pleased to be appointed. But why me? "We're looking for someone who strongly supports Governor Reagan and is also a member of the Sierra Club," he said. (Although I'd been a member of the Sierra Club for about fifteen years at that point, the organization had been turning hard left recently and I resigned not many months later.)

The TRPA's governing board passed on a variety of zoning matters, including variances and permits for such things as casinos and housing developments. Each governor had one appointee (all the other members were ex officio). We were paid a modest per diem on meeting days and were reimbursed for travel expenses, but otherwise worked gratis. I was lobbied heavily by both sides in every dispute, yet I never once was instructed by Governor Reagan or his staff as to my votes.

At the beginning of 1974, Reagan's last year in Sacramento, I was invited to join his senior staff with the title of Assistant to the Governor and Director of Public Affairs. That meant resigning from the TRPA board (he did not want his staff members also to hold appointments).

A few days after I had begun work, I remarked to Mike Deaver—the governor's director of administration, who had joined Reagan early in his first term—how smoothly the place seemed to run. "Morale is high, the teamwork is impressive, everything works professionally and efficiently," I said. He smiled and said, "Remember, we've had seven years' practice."

In addition to my regular duties, it fell to me—on my own time—to check out various post governorship offers that were coming in to Ronald Reagan. One Monday morning, I went into his office on some matter and he told me that his friend Efrem Zimbalist, Jr., had related how pleased he was with a syndicated radio program Zimbalist was doing with one Harry O'Connor, a producer in Hollywood. It seems that O'Connor thought there was a market also for a conservative commentary program and wanted to talk with Reagan about it. "Check it out when you're in Los Angeles, will you?" the governor asked me.

At the same time, newspaper syndicates were expressing interest in a column by Reagan. I related all this to Deaver, who said that the governor's scheduling office (which reported to him) had been receiving a number of speaking invitations for dates after his term would expire, January 5, 1975. He said, "We're sending them pro forma letters saying they will hear from his private office about the invitation, but the fact is there's no private office and unless someone does something about it soon, next January the mailbags will be coming through the door and the telephone will be ringing off the hook at the Reagans' home with only them and the housekeeper on hand."

At this time, I was on leave from my small public relations/ public affairs firm and mentioned that, at the close of the governor's term, I planned to return to it. I invited Mike to join me. "But I don't know anything about the public relations business," he said. "What do you think you've been doing the last seven-plus years?" I replied. That was the beginning of what would become Deaver & Hannaford, Inc.

One Saturday in October, he and I flew to Los Angeles and presented the Reagans with our plan. We had talked with several of our colleagues and asked them if they would be interested in joining such a firm if it were to become a reality. They all agreed. We had prepared income and expense budgets. A small cadre of people with whom the Reagans were familiar would do in microcosm what a staff of 105 in the Governor's Office had been doing: scheduling, advance, research, communications support, correspondence, administration. The Reagans approved the plan and the new firm opened on the first Monday in January 1975, in the Tishman Building on Wilshire Boulevard in the Westwood section of Los Angeles.

Ronald Reagan's personal office was inside our suite. Mrs. Reagan oversaw its furnishing. It looked much like his corner office in the capitol in Sacramento, with most of the same furniture (which belonged to Mr. Reagan) and pictures. Only the view was different. Instead of Capitol Park, it looked out toward Santa Catalina Island offshore and south at the airplanes coming and going at Los Angeles International Airport. That was to be his office until 1980 when he was in the midst of the presidential campaign.

Our contract called for one of us to travel with him on his speaking tours and other trips. Mike, who oversaw logistics, scheduling, and political liaison, took more of those trips than I did. Research and editorial support were among my duties, and in that pre-personal-and-laptop-computer/cellular-phone age, I had to stick to home base a good part of the time.

In the 1976 presidential primary campaign, we were both on the road with Reagan all of the time. Our firm had other clients, but we had a vice president in Los Angeles who could attend to their needs while we were away.

When it came time to make plans for the 1980 campaign (in late 1978), the situation had changed. Our company had opened a Washington office in February 1977, and had more clients and a larger staff. Both Mike and I couldn't go into the campaign. After much discussion, we decided that Mike would join the Reagan Exploratory Committee in March 1979, when it opened for business at an office near the airport. He would devote about 95 percent of his time to the committee and the rest to the company. The allotment of my time would be the reverse. Ronald Reagan intended to remain a noncandidate for as much of the year as possible, so a liaison would be needed between his office and the committee. Our plan was that, upon Reagan's announcement of his candidacy in November, Mike would go on leave from the company and go into the campaign full-time. I would stay out to run the company.

It worked out differently. About two weeks after the announcement in New York City, John Sears, the campaign director, threatened to resign if Mike continued in the campaign. (Sears was intent on consolidating decision-making in his own hands.) Mike withdrew. He came back to Deaver & Hannaford full-time. The formal campaign began in January. Sears's strategy was to have Reagan do minimal on-the-ground campaigning in Iowa, whose caucuses would be the first test of strength. Reagan was ahead in the polls and Sears was concerned that appearances with the several other Republican hopefuls would raise their profiles too much.

Reagan lost the Iowa caucuses to George Bush. I read the news in South Africa, where I was on a long-planned trip at the time. As soon as I returned, I called Ed Meese (the sole remaining Californian in a senior campaign position) to ask if I could be of any help as a volunteer. He asked me to come to Andover, Massachusetts (where the Reagans and staff were staying during the New Hampshire primary), to help prepare Governor Reagan for the all-candidate nationally televised debate the following week. I did, and soon found myself part of a small circle that concluded that Sears's strategy had failed, that a schism in the staff had to be healed, and that Sears and his key people had to be replaced.

William Casey, later to become Reagan's CIA director, agreed to take on the management of the campaign. Over the next several days, by long-distance conference telephone calls, the group of four or five of us worked out the plan for the transfer of management. It was carried out the afternoon of the New Hampshire primary, before the election results were known.

As a result, I found myself traveling with the campaign for most of the primary season, as the press secretary for the first trip (the previous press secretary had left with Sears), then as communications adviser. Mike, meanwhile, had been asked to be Ronald Reagan's personal representative on his executive committee (an expanded version of the old Reagan kitchen cabinet).

For the Republican National Convention in Detroit that July, I was asked to take charge of research and writing. I organized a team of writers for the dozens of assignments that would need to be carried out and had, as my special assignment, working with Ronald Reagan on his acceptance speech.

Mike arrived in Detroit with the Reagans and, as soon as the convention was over, we returned to our original plan. He participated in the general election campaign full-time, and, except for a few volunteer activities, I stayed out and ran the company. After the election, Mike went to work at the White House as deputy chief of staff and I continued with the company. I enjoyed several opportunities to help the Reagan administration, including membership on the United States Information Agency's Public Relations Advisory Committee, and serving as a consultant to the President's Commission on Privatization.

From 1989, the year President Reagan retired from the White House to his home and office in Los Angeles, until 1994, the year in which he announced to the nation that he had Alzheimer's disease, I had the pleasure of assisting him on a number of his speeches and newspaper articles. On his trips to Central and Eastern Europe in those years, he was greeted as a hero, and he had a number of speaking opportunities that allowed him to reflect on the momentous events in which he had been such an important figure.

Over the years that I worked with and for Ronald Reagan and traveled to various parts of the world with him, I always found him to be in private as he was in public: courteous, patient, affable, and good-humored. He had a high boiling point. I rarely saw him angry, and then it was usually over some politician's abandonment of professed principle.

Reagan had worked out his own set of principles over a period of time and stuck to them, although he was not dogmatic when it came to negotiating or dealing with the realities of political compromise. As he once said of his landmark welfare reforms in California in the early 1970s, "If I can get seventy percent of what I want from a legislature controlled by the opposition, I'll take my chances on getting the other thirty when they see how well it works."

It is too early to fully assess the lasting impact of Ronald Reagan's work. Certainly, contemporary historians, being part of Reagan's time, are too close to the picture to do it. More time must pass. My guess is, that in the fullness of time, the historical consensus will be that he has been one of the most important figures of the twentieth century. Meanwhile, you, the reader, can begin to form your own judgment through the experiences of the men and women you will meet in this book. Each has his or her favorite recollections of Ronald Reagan. They tell their stories in their own words, the sum total of which I hope will give you a clear picture of the character of the remarkable man who became the fortieth President of the United States.

—Peter Hannaford
Washington, D.C.

ACKNOWLEDGMENTS

My thanks go to a number of people who have made this book possible: to Bill Adler, my literary agent, whose idea inspired the project; Zachary Schisgal, my editor at William Morrow, for his patience, good cheer, and good advice; my wife, Irene, for the many hours she spent transcribing taped interviews; Nancy Reagan for her support; and all the men and women who gave generously of their time to tell me their recollections.

CONTENTS

INTRODUCTION

Radio sportscaster, film and television star, union leader, thirty-third governor of California, fortieth President of the United States. Ronald Reagan, who never regarded himself as a professional politician, had several distinct careers, and each contributed to his success and popularity. Over time, he became known as the Great Communicator, with whom all other public speakers were—and still are—compared. More than a speechmaker, he pursued policies and actions that, together, provided the catalyst for bringing the cold war to an end (Margaret Thatcher said of him, "Ronald Reagan won the cold war single-handed, without firing a shot!"). At the same time, he was leading the nation's longest-running peacetime economic expansion. And, he gave gallantry a new definition, not once, but three times (when he caught a would-be assassin's bullet, when he was operated on for cancer, and when he announced to the world that he had Alzheimer's disease).

He was the scourge of liberals, leftists, statists, and socialists, who realized that he had unleashed an unstoppable force to take power away from Washington and put it in the hands of the states, counties, communities, families, and individuals.

Ronald Wilson Reagan was born February 6, 1911, in Tampico, Illinois, the second son of Jack and Nelle Reagan. A blizzard had just dumped ten inches of snow on the small town where Jack worked at a general store. The family lived in a flat above a bakery on Main Street. Jack called his little son "the fat little Dutchman" because of his robust appearance—and "Dutch" became the nickname by which many of Ronald Reagan's friends from his youthful years knew him.

While he was still a toddler, the family began a series of moves—all in Illinois—as Jack changed jobs: Chicago, Galesburg, Monmouth, back to Tampico (where they lived above the general store where Jack had worked before), and finally to Dixon in December 1920. Warren Harding had just been elected President. It was in Dixon that the future President finished elementary and high school. Football became his passion, and, in his high school summers, he was also a lifeguard on the nearby Rock River.

It was in Dixon that he was baptized, along with his brother, Neil, in a ceremony that included total immersion (symbolizing the death, burial, and resurrection of Christ). Nelle's denomination, the Disciples of Christ, or Christian Church (a Presbyterian offshoot), did not believe in infant baptism, so this ceremony for the eleven-year-old Ronald represented a conscious commitment. Throughout his life, he believed that God had a plan for each person. His deep and abiding faith came from his devout mother.

His father, though never a success in business and often struggling with a drinking problem, had a resiliency in times of adversity and a sunny disposition that became part of his younger son's personality as he grew.

In 1928, he entered Eureka College, one hundred miles from Dixon, a 220-student liberal arts school connected with the Christian Church. He received a modest athletic scholarship and earned money by washing dishes. He won letters in track and was a lifeguard in summers, but his passion was football. Added to this was his activity in the drama club and student government.

When he graduated in June 1932, the country was deep into the Great Depression. "Dutch" Reagan decided he would become a radio announcer and tried to find a job at every station in Chicago—without luck. Then he set out to canvass the countryside around Dixon. He got his first job at WOC in Davenport, Iowa, across the Mississippi River from Rock Island, Illinois, after re-creating—before the microphone—the fourth quarter of a Eureka College game of the previous season. His audition won him the chance to broadcast a game from Iowa City the next Saturday for "five dollars and bus fare." He so impressed the station's crusty manager that he was hired to do the next three games for double the amount.

That fall, Dutch Reagan cast his first presidential vote—for Franklin Delano Roosevelt. Reagan's father was a staunch Democrat, the New Deal had great appeal, and, as Reagan noted later, FDR promised "to reduce the size of the federal government and cut the budget by 25 percent."

Meanwhile, his sportscasting stints turned into a regular job, first as staff announcer and then—the following spring—a transfer to the owner's other station, powerful clear-channel WHO in Des Moines, the state capital. There, he earned a reputation and a following for his colorful re-creation of Chicago Cubs baseball games (the information came in by wire, without description, so the "color" had to be added by the announcer). In later years, Reagan regaled listeners with stories from his radio days.

His adolescent interest in acting had never left him. By the winter of 1936–37, he was seriously thinking about the possibility of working in films. A trip to California's Santa Catalina Island the next spring to cover the Cubs' spring training gave him the opportunity to look into the matter firsthand. A friend arranged a screen test at Warner Brothers. The following morning, he left for Des Moines and, on his first day back at the radio station, received a telegram from Warner Brothers offering him a seven-year contract at $200 a week, starting June 1, 1937.

Fifty-three feature-length films later, Ronald Reagan had a well-established reputation as a solid player (though rarely the one who got the girl). He gained another of his nicknames, "The Gipper," from his role in Knute Rockne—All American, in which he played the courageous, dying George Gipp. He considered his role as Drake McHugh in King's Row (1942) his best. Ann

Sheridan was his costar. The McHugh character has both legs amputated by an evil doctor and when he awakes proclaims, "Where's the rest of me"—a line that became the title of a Reagan autobiography in the early 1960s.

Long an Army reservist in the cavalry (where he learned to ride), Reagan was called to active duty as a second lieutenant in April 1942 at Fort Mason, in San Francisco. His nearsightedness kept him from going overseas, but he was soon transferred to the Army Air Force's First Motion Picture Unit in southern California which produced training films at the old Hal Roach studios (dubbed "Fort Roach").

He returned to his civilian career following his Army discharge in 1945. The next year, he was elected vice president of the Screen Actors Guild, and became president in 1947. He held that office for the next four years (and again in 1959–60), a time of turmoil in Hollywood, as Communists sought to take over several unions. The fight to keep them from doing so occupied much of Reagan's time, as did SAG contract negotiations with the studios. In later years, he credited his SAG experience with helping him develop the negotiating skills he used so deftly in elective politics and summit meetings.

He and actress Jane Wyman were married in 1940, but divorced eight years later. In March 1952, Ronald Reagan and Nancy Davis were married. She gave up her promising film career to be a wife and mother.

In 1954, Reagan signed a contract with General Electric to become the host of a new weekly half-hour television anthology, *General Electric Theater*. Broadcast live, over the next eight years it featured many of Hollywood's top stars. Reagan himself starred from time to time and he and Nancy played opposite one another several times.

His contract called for him to visit GE factories around the country. He met with workers on the factory floor and addressed them at shift changes. It was in that setting that he developed his technique of giving brief opening remarks about values and the country's problems, then shifting to taking questions ("a dialogue, not a monologue," as he put it). Politically, his views were moving from New Deal liberal to conservativism. His father-in-law, Dr. Loyal Davis, a prominent Chicago neurosurgeon, was an important influence, and Earl Dunckel, the GE executive who traveled with Reagan on the plant tours, constantly argued the conservative point of view with him.

Increasingly, in his appearances at GE factories and in speeches to civic groups, he focused on the menace of the Communist movement around the world. Politically, he made the move to the Republican party in 1962. That year, Congressman H. Allen Smith and some political friends called on Reagan to sound him out about running for governor, but he declined. *General Electric Theater* had just ended its run and he had become host of *Death Valley Days*.

On October 27, 1964, Ronald Reagan's life would change forever. To help the presidential candidacy of his friend Senator Barry Goldwater (and at the behest of his own brother, Neil, an advertising agency executive in charge of the Goldwater campaign's advertising), Reagan filmed an electrifying speech titled "A Time for Choosing" for release on national television that night. The speech raised approximately $1 million for the Goldwater campaign in its final days. More important, it brought to the political stage a charismatic new star.

Pressed by friends to run for governor of California in 1966, he agreed to travel the state to "test the water." He faced, and defeated, San Francisco's respected Mayor George Christopher in the Republican primary that year and went on to defeat popular two-term Governor Edmund G. "Pat" Brown by a million votes.

Dedicated to bringing the state's burgeoning government under control, the new governor embarked on a "cut, squeeze, and trim" program, using citizen task forces to identify potential savings. Required by its constitution to have a balanced budget, California had nevertheless been running in the red under Governor Reagan's predecessor. Reagan had bowed to the necessity of raising taxes to cure the problem, but promised that as soon as surpluses developed and reserves were created, he would return the rest to the taxpayers. And, over the course of his eight years as governor, he returned some $5 billion to the taxpayers.

The state's welfare system was galloping out of control until Reagan and his administration devised a massive reform program. He personally negotiated the plan with leaders in the Democratic-controlled state legislature.

On the environmental front, he is credited with stopping an all-weather highway from being built across the spectacular Minarets area of the Sierra Nevada mountains and for preventing construction of a huge new federal dam (Dos Rios) that would have flooded Indian burial grounds and farms in Round Valley in the northern part of California.

In 1968, his second year in office, Reagan led the California delegation to the Republican convention in Miami as its "favorite son." Senator William Knowland wanted instead to nominate Reagan as a *bona fide* candidate and did so at the last minute. While that effort did not succeed, it demonstrated that Reagan had the beginnings of a national constituency.

In 1973, he proposed a state constitutional amendment to limit the percentage of the people's aggregate income the state could take to run its affairs. Although the ballot measure ultimately lost, it drew national attention and triggered the tax revolt that swept the country later in the decade.

Although there were no term limits at the time, he said that two terms were enough and did not run for a third in 1974. In early January 1975, his second term concluded and he returned to private life, but a busy one, with a daily radio commentary program, a twice-weekly newspaper column, and a steady round of speaking tours. His popularity on leaving office was high and many were urging him to challenge Gerald Ford for the presidential nomination in 1976.

In November 1975, he announced that he would enter the contest. Although he lost the early primaries, he came back strongly in the later ones, with Ford and Reagan essentially neck and neck as they arrived at the Republican National Convention in Kansas City. The matter was decided over a vote on rules the night before the actual nomination voting. Reagan lost it narrowly, and President Ford later lost to Jimmy Carter.

Reagan returned to his media activities but, not long after

Carter assumed office, found growing support for a 1980 candidacy. This time George Bush was his principal rival, but Reagan swept the early primaries and went to the convention in Detroit a solid winner, inviting Bush to join the ticket as vice presidential candidate.

Carter's people, as had Pat Brown's years before, assumed that Reagan would be an easy candidate to defeat, because they underestimated his ability to connect with the values of large numbers of voters. Reagan only had to disprove the image his detractors had fashioned for him; that is, that he was a warlike extremist. When, in one of the campaign debates, Carter went into a litany to conjure up that image, Reagan said simply, "There you go again." It was a turning point.

Reagan won by 51 to 41 percent (with 7 for John Anderson), with the electoral vote 489–49. He won all but six states and the District of Columbia.

Reagan had campaigned on three themes: reduce the tax burden; restore the nation's armed forces; and curb the growth of government. Once in office, he set about to accomplish all three with single-mindedness. By July 1981, a sweeping cut in income tax rates had been accomplished (with the help of a number of "Boll Weevil" Democrats in Congress); his Peace Through Strength defense buildup was well under way; and a range of government programs were being challenged as to their size and effectiveness.

Although the nation sustained a recession in 1982—the result of pre-Reagan policies—recovery began late that year with an economic expansion that proved, by the time he left office in January 1989, to be the longest peacetime one in the nation's history. Some nineteen million jobs and tens of thousands of new businesses were created. Inflation—which had routinely been 10 percent or more in the 1970s, was wrestled down to the 3- to 4-percent range.

Determined to roll back communism, Reagan in June 1982—in an address to the British parliament—announced what came to be known as the Reagan Doctrine. It was the obverse of the Brezhnev Doctrine, which held that once a nation had gone

Communist, it would never change. Instead, Reagan called for a "crusade for freedom" and pledged that the United States would support those who were fighting against communism "wherever we find them." In his book *Speaking My Mind,* he wrote:

> I am amazed that our national leaders had not philosophically and intellectually taken on the principles of Marxism-Leninism. We were always too worried we would offend the Soviets if we struck at anything so basic. Well, so what? Marxist-Leninist thought is an empty cupboard. Everyone knew it by the 1980s. but no one was saying it. I decided to articulate a few of these things.

His candor was even sharper the following year when, on March 8, he addressed the National Association of Evangelicals and described the Soviet Union as an "evil empire." Pundits and critics gasped in horror. He was roundly criticized, but once the Soviet Union disintegrated a few years later and its evil ways were exposed to full view, Reagan was once again vindicated.

Reagan's characterization of the Soviet Union was no spur-of-the-moment applause line. Knowing from intelligence reports the shaky character of the Soviet economy, he had decided not only to rebuild U.S. armed forces, but also to provide the political will to develop a Strategic Defense Initiative to deter Soviet long-range missiles. He knew the Soviets could not match the United States in such an endeavor without bankrupting themselves. His counterpart, Mikhail Gorbachev, knew it, too, which is why at their 1986 summit in Reykjavik, Iceland, Gorbachev made U.S. abandonment of SDI his price for an arms reduction agreement. Reagan did not back down. Indeed, his administration persuaded the German government to station cruise missiles in Germany, effectively neutralizing another major category of Soviet missiles that would have been used in any attack on Western Europe.

In 1987, in an address before the Brandenburg Gate and the Berlin Wall, he said, "Mr. Gorbachev, open this gate! Mr. Gorbachev, tear down this wall!" It happened a little over two years later. In May 1988, at his final summit, in Moscow, President

Reagan slaked the thirst for democracy that glasnost had created among the Russian people when he addressed the students at Moscow State University and invited Soviet dissidents to speak their minds at the U.S. embassy.

There is little doubt now that Ronald Reagan's calculated plan to challenge and roll back communism was the catalyst that led to the demise of the Soviet Union and its orchestrated international Marxist movement. After leaving office in January 1989, he traveled to Germany, Poland, and Russia, where he was greeted as a hero.

Beyond his specific accomplishments on the world stage, Ronald Reagan gave the nation something it badly needed: a restoration of self-confidence and pride. His civility and good humor combined to defuse many a confrontation and win him enduring popularity as a leader.

KENNETH ADELMAN

DIRECTOR, U.S. ARMS CONTROL AND
DISARMAMENT AGENCY, 1983–87

"What Gorbachev realized was that Reagan was dead serious about the SDI."

During the nearly five years he headed the ACDA, Ken Adelman accompanied President Reagan to the Geneva and Reykjavik summits, where initiatives to reduce and eliminate nuclear weapons had their beginnings. Before that, he had been deputy U.S. representative to the United Nations. A nationally syndicated columnist, he is the author of four books and is vice president of the Institute for Contemporary Studies. He holds a doctorate from Georgetown University.

In November 1985, the United States and the Soviet Union had their first summit in some seven years. Therefore, it was the first both for Ronald Reagan and Mikhail Gorbachev. It occurred at a time when there was a deep suspicion between the two countries. The Kremlin had been behind a major campaign to show Reagan as a dangerous man and themselves as peace-loving.

Reagan spent most of the morning with Gorbachev at a house near the shore of Lake Geneva, establishing his relationship with Gorbachev. When he returned to his own villa, he asked us to wait in the dining room while he went to the rest room. When he joined us, he had a big grin on his face. We began to realize that while he was in the rest room, he had taken his left arm out of his jacket sleeve, so now the sleeve was hanging limply. He looked down, grabbed the sleeve, and said, "Where's my arm? It was here this morning, before I met Gorbachev."

When we stopped laughing, one of us asked, "Well, Mr. President, what did you think of him?" He said, "Let me tell you, he's sure a new kind of Soviet leader." I said to myself, "Oh-oh, he's fallen 'in love' already." I was fearful he was losing his anti-Communist ardor. That fear was quickly dissipated by his subsequent sessions with Gorbachev, when he was strong and forthright about Afghanistan and other world problems. Typical of him, he was right about Gorbachev being a new type of leader. I thought he handled the Geneva summit perfectly.

Reykjavik, in October 1986, was entirely different. By then, there was even more tension between the United States and the Soviet Union. Gorbachev, at the end of a three- or four-page very nasty letter to the President, put in a paragraph saying the two of them should get together to *prepare* for a summit.

That was a peculiar proposal. He suggested either London or Reykjavik in ten days' time. Geneva and previous summits had been months in preparation. Although this was very abrupt, Reagan said he would like to do it. London was ruled out because of the complication of the European leaders getting involved and other unavoidable obligations. At Reykjavik, on the other hand, we could hold the summit without any such distractions.

President Reagan accepted. We had been assured by the Soviet ambassador in Washington, by our own ambassador in Moscow, and by CIA and State Department experts that all Gorbachev wanted was a "howdy-hello" photo op—nothing very substantive. As a result, we didn't prepare for much more.

On our first day in Reykjavik—the day before the summit opened—Reagan seemed somewhat out of sorts. It may have been the time-zone change or his concerns about problems with the Senate over arms issues, which we needed for leverage. Yet, by the next morning—Friday, October 10, as I recall—he was back in very good shape.

Gorbachev came in with a packet of proposals. He proposed drastic changes in nuclear arsenals. The President turned the proposals over to those of us who had accompanied him to negotiate—all Saturday night, as it turned out—with a delegation headed by a five-star Soviet marshal who had been a World War II hero.

We briefed the President at seven the next morning in the bubble (the secure room of the U.S. embassy in Reykjavik). He met with Gorbachev throughout that morning. The summit was supposed to end at noon, but they kept talking into the afternoon. We in his team stayed on the second floor of Hofti House (which was reputed to be haunted), while he and Gorbachev met on the first floor. Reagan came upstairs frequently to show us papers that Gorbachev had presented for discussion. There were just the two of them, plus Secretary of State George Shultz, Soviet Foreign Minister Eduard Shevardnadze, and two translators.

On each of these visits upstairs, Reagan would discuss with us the U.S. response to Gorbachev's proposals. Finally, he said he was going back down with his last offer. He went to the door of our meeting room, then came back and asked the six or seven of us there, "Is there anybody here who thinks I'm giving away too much?" There wasn't, and he headed downstairs.

Gorbachev surprised Reagan by offering to eliminate all the medium-range (INF) missiles in Europe and to greatly reduce the Soviets' strategic arsenal—yet with a string attached: Reagan had to give up the SDI (Strategic Defense Initiative). That was Gorbachev's hidden agenda, crippling our SDI. He said simply that the SDI should be confined to a "laboratory." The thrust of Reagan's response was this: Would you fly in an airplane that was confined to a laboratory, that hadn't been tried out? I wouldn't, and most people wouldn't. It depends on your definition of "laboratory." If you include using all of space, that's fine. We can buy that. But, if you mean just a laboratory in a building somewhere, we can't accept that or just test a defense program with a space component.

They talked back and forth about the meaning of "laboratory." Gorbachev meant a room at, say, the Livermore Lab. Reagan meant the universe. There was no way to square that, so Reagan decided he had had enough and walked Gorbachev out to their cars. I was close behind them. You could see on Reagan's face that he was very angry about the breakdown. Gorbachev turned to him and said, "I don't know what else we could have done." Reagan replied, "You could have said yes."

We went back to the U.S. ambassador's house where the President was staying. He was still upset. Shultz held a press conference, where he looked as if a horse had just kicked him in the stomach.

My view of the summit was quite simple—and different. I felt that once we resumed negotiations in Geneva, it would be impossible for the Soviet delegation to claim they could not accept the idea of no SS-20 missiles in Europe; not after Gorbachev had said yes to that particular item. Gorbachev had said, in effect, "This package is fine, so long as you give us the SDI limitations (i.e., laboratory only) for me to market it at home." In subsequent negotiations, the Soviets agreed to eliminate the SS-20s.

Reagan's angry departure—and especially the disastrous Shultz press conference—caused worldwide headlines and static in briefing allies and Congress. All of that took the focus away from what had really been accomplished. What Gorbachev realized was that Reagan was dead serious about the SDI. And, as a result, the Soviets became serious about an INF (intermediate nuclear forces) treaty, which was signed a little over a year later. That was a tremendous accomplishment, for the treaty was the first agreement to eliminate a whole class of nuclear weapons; it was the first arms control agreement to really help the security of Western Europe in a measurable way. Also at Reykjavik, we made more progress on START (the Strategic Arms Reduction Talks) than we had in the whole preceding four years.

Reagan handled the negotiations at Reykjavik very well. In retrospect, I think he should have told Shultz to tell the press it had been a great triumph (because it was)—that it had been a hell of a week's end—instead of letting the press concentrate on the short-term flare-up and the seeming failure to agree. Ultimately, the success at Reykjavik paid off handsomely.

The Strategic Defense Initiative is one of the elements that broke the back of the Soviet Union. The deployment of the Pershing cruise missiles in Germany in 1983 also contributed greatly. As for the SDI, Gorbachev would have been smart to say, "If you want to waste a lot of money on this program, go right ahead." Instead, they went crazy over the SDI. About three quarters of their propaganda budget in 1984, '85, and '86 was directed solely against it. It was driving them nuts. Some in Congress considered this program a waste of our money. I testified to the effect that if it was such a silly program, why were the Soviets so upset about it? Reagan's view was that developing the SDI was the right to thing to do. It would show the Soviets they could never keep up with us. He was right.

RICHARD V. ALLEN
PRESIDENTIAL NATIONAL SECURITY ADVISER,
1981–82

"Both incidents that took place on that trip signify to me a man who set goals for himself that he would swear to fulfill if he had the power to do so. And, of course, as President of the United States, he gained that power."

Richard Allen was President Reagan's first assistant to the president for national security affairs. From 1977 to 1980, he was Mr. Reagan's chief foreign policy adviser. He is a Distinguished Fellow of the Heritage Foundation and chairman of its Asian Studies Center. In the Nixon White House, he served as deputy assistant to the President and deputy executive director of the Council on International Economic Policy. A founding member of the United States National Committee for Pacific Basin Economic Cooperation, he is today chairman of an international consulting firm with offices in Washington, D.C., and Seoul, Korea.

From my point of view, the opportunity to work closely with Ronald Reagan represents a highlight of my life. I was first attracted to his character and forthrightness when he was running for the Republican nomination in 1976. It was not until later, in early 1977, that I came to know him. He had lost that nomination to Gerald Ford and Ford had lost to Jimmy Carter. A friend on Ronald Reagan's staff arranged for me to call on Reagan in California. I came away from that meeting convinced I had been in the presence of the most powerful political figure in my lifetime.

That meeting led to a progressively deeper involvement with Reagan, including some travel with him to both Europe and Asia in 1978. Those trips were in preparation for a possible run for the presidency in 1980. One aspect of that travel was his first visit to Germany, in December 1978. On that particular trip were planted the seeds of some important policy measures that were to blossom in his presidency. On that trip, which also included England and France, there developed in conversations with Reagan the notion of what were to become the Caribbean Basin Initiative and the North American Free Trade Agreement (which in those days we called the North American Accord).

The concepts reflected not only his strong belief in removing barriers to international trade as a key to widespread prosperity, but also the importance he attached to harmony among all the nations of the Americas. Although the North American Accord took shape only in rudimentary form during that trip, it was later refined to become a component of his November 1979 speech announcing his candidacy for the presidency the following year.

Once in the White House, he made this one of the centerpieces of his administration. It was during those years that democracy in Latin America began to flower. The fact that there is widespread democratic capitalism throughout Latin America today is at least partly due to Ronald Reagan's enlightened policy.

Another of the Reagan administration's most dramatic policy initiatives—the Reagan Doctrine to roll back communism—was also born on that 1978 trip. It was in Berlin. The Reagans, Peter Hannaford, our wives, and I and a nervous fellow from our consulate passed through Checkpoint Charlie into East Berlin to the Alexanderplatz, a prominent spot. We got out of the car and began to walk around. At that moment, an incident occurred that set Ronald Reagan's blood to boiling. Two East German *volkspolizei* had stopped a shopper. They made him place his bags on the ground and produce his identification; then they searched his bags. Reagan was livid, and muttered that this was an outrage. It was clear from his reaction that he was determined to one day go about removing such a system.

On our return toward West Berlin, we traveled by several points of the Wall, including a spot where an incident had occurred several years before. It involved a young boy who succeeded in passing through the first set of barriers surrounding the Wall, but became entangled in barbed wire. His comrades had escaped ahead of him into West Berlin, but this boy, Peter Fechter, being the last over, was detected by searchlights and shot by an East German guard. He stayed on that fence for some hours before he died and his body was removed. Ronald Reagan listened to his episode with fascination and, again, anger whirled within him. It was clear he placed a high priority on seeing that Wall come down one day. Years later, in 1987, as President of the United States, he would stand in front of that Wall and demand, "Mr. Gorbachev, tear down this wall."

I'll never forget these incidents because they proved to me that Ronald Reagan was a man with long-term vision and the courage to develop policies to match it. Of course, with him it was not just a matter of tearing down the Berlin Wall, but of tearing down the entire Communist system that he despised intensely. He came to the presidency with a strong bias against totalitarians and was intent on using his position of leadership to lead a coalition of forces against Communist regimes wherever they ruled. He wanted to undermine them and ultimately make them crumble. He set out to create difficulties for them, to induce weaknesses that could be exploited so they might collapse of their own weight.

Some will argue that Reagan's policies were not the proximate cause for the collapse of the Communist systems in Central and

Eastern Europe and the Soviet Union. I believe they were. Most people, as they reflect on the Reagan administration, will recognize his great contribution toward changing the map of the world, freeing people who were, in fact, enslaved, and making the development of democratic systems possible in those countries. Certainly, he provided the catalyst and, certainly, that is the view in the former Soviet-bloc countries where Reagan today is regarded as a hero.

MARTIN ANDERSON
PRESIDENTIAL DOMESTIC AND ECONOMIC POLICY
ADVISER, SCHOLAR, AUTHOR

"I have never seen before or since a man with such political courage."

Chief domestic and policy adviser to President Ronald Reagan in 1981–82, Martin Anderson was senior policy adviser to candidate Reagan in his 1976 and 1980 presidential campaigns. Earlier, he had served in the Nixon administration in several positions, following an academic career at the Massachusetts Institute of Technology and Columbia University. He has served on a number of economic, defense, and foreign-policy-related federal commissions and boards over the last two decades. He is a senior fellow at the Hoover Institution at Stanford University and is the author of six books, the latest of which are Impostors in the Temple *(1992) and* Revolution *(1988).*

Today, looking back over Ronald Reagan's presidency, there is no correlation between what he accomplished and much of the current conventional wisdom about him. One hundred years from now, however, after the political dust of the twentieth century has settled, the historians of that time will write that Ronald Reagan was one of the greatest American Presidents. He will be remembered for three things: ending the cold war with the Soviet Union and, along with it, the threat of a global nuclear war; defeating Marxism/communism; and presiding over one of the greatest economic expansions in history.

Working for him, one of the first things that struck me about him was his high intelligence. I can recall many times sitting or traveling with him, introducing an idea or essay or memorandum. He would grasp its essence almost immediately; then, sometimes weeks or months later, he would interpret it and weave the relevant material into a speech or statement of his own.

It is not widely known, but he was a superb speech writer. Often, he would sit down with a long yellow pad and write them out longhand. Unless circumstances called for the use of a Tele-PrompTer, he'd do what he called "carding" his speech. Using four-by-six-inch index cards, he would write the text in capital letters, employing his own shorthand, which consisted largely of dropping vowels and articles. Then, when he had the whole speech on fifteen or twenty cards, he would put an elastic band around them and tuck them in his pocket, ready to use. He would walk up to the lectern with his whole speech in one small packet. He would just reach in, lay it down, and glance briefly at each card. While he seemed to be giving an extemporaneous speech, he was actually reading his cards.

I remember one time asking him why he used this technique. He said, "You can't give a major policy speech unless you have the facts straight and the policy ideas worked out. You've got to write it out. Also, people don't like to see a speaker reading a speech from a text."

He had extraordinary judgment. Going after a major policy change, crafting a practical policy initiative, and sticking with it is an accomplishment. I think the biggest one of all was the question of the Soviet empire and the threat they posed to the

United States with their nuclear weapons. If you go back and look at certain events, you see the continuity and persistence of his ideas.

For example, in 1983 he came out with a speech announcing the Strategic Defense Initiative. He even surprised his secretaries of state and defense with it. The common reaction was "Oh, my God, this is spur-of-the-moment; he doesn't know what he's talking about." Detractors called it "Star Wars."

I began to trace its beginnings. It began earlier, but the first time I heard him talk about it was at the 1976 Republican convention in Kansas City. After he had lost the nomination to Gerald Ford, President Ford called him down to the floor for an impromptu speech. He had no notes. At the end of that speech, he talked about the most important thing to him. It wasn't tax cuts, balancing the budget, or welfare reform; it was the contents of a letter he had written for a time capsule that would be opened on the three-hundredth anniversary of the founding of Los Angeles. Here is the climax of it:

> We live in a world in which the great powers have poised and aimed at each other horrible missiles of destruction that can, in a matter of minutes, arrive in each other's country and destroy virtually the civilized world we live in.
>
> . . . suddenly it dawned on me. Those who would read this letter a hundred years from now will know whether those missiles were fired. They will know whether we met our challenge. Whether they have the freedoms that we have known up until now will depend on what we do. Will they look back with appreciation and say, "Thank God for those people in 1976 who headed off that loss of freedom, who kept our world from nuclear destruction"?

That is a powerful statement of what he's all about. Even before he became President, he began to develop the idea of Strategic Arms Reduction Talks—START. One day in 1979, Dick Allen had arranged for a number of experts to brief Reagan in his office in Los Angeles on the proposed SALT II treaty. Now "SALT" stood for Strategic Arms Limitation Talks. Suddenly, Reagan stopped the discussion and said, "We ought to have a START treaty. Instead of just limiting the rate of growth of strategic arms, we should reduce them." At that time, the most radical thing on the horizon was the leftists' call for a nuclear "freeze," and here was our candidate calling for a reduction in arms! He never lost track of that goal and kept driving for it until he reached it.

That summer of 1979 he had visited NORAD, our missile-tracking nerve center deep in the Rocky Mountains. The lesson he came away with from that visit was that the President has two alternatives, both bad: Accept a missile attack and do nothing, or engage in massive retaliation and start a global nuclear war. What we needed, he said, was a third choice—missile defense.

Fast-forward four years, with many meetings in between. I recall him meeting with various experts, during which his questions were about technical feasibility and the cost of a missile defense. So, what appeared to some as a spur-of-the-moment notion when he introduced it as SDI, he had actually been planning for a long time.

Another very important event in 1983 took place two weeks after the SDI speech. This came to be called "The Evil Empire Speech," because that is the term he used in it to describe the Soviet Union. In it he said, "While they preach supremacy of the state, declaring omnipotence over man, and predict domination over everyone on earth, they have the focus of evil over the modern world. . . ." He described the struggle between the USSR and the United States as a "struggle between right and wrong, good and evil." That was much stronger than was reported by the news media.

While he was denouncing the Soviet empire and moving forward with the SDI, he was secretly negotiating with Yuri Andropov, then the Soviet leader. He wrote personal letters that were hand-delivered by then-National Security Adviser Bill Clark to the Soviet ambassador, who would pass them on to Andropov. Then, Andropov would write back. Reagan was leaving no stone unturned in his search for long-term peace.

One of the great myths that has been perpetrated is that Reagan was at the mercy of his advisers, a so-called empty vessel. On the contrary, he had a clear policy vision carefully mapped out in his mind. Indeed, he was better at it than we were.

His courage and determination came through time after time. In 1976, after he had lost five straight primaries, he was badgered by the press and pressured by various Republican bigwigs to quit the race as he arrived in North Carolina for his final campaign trip there. It looked very bleak. Anyone else would have quit, but not Ronald Reagan. He took a deep breath, said to those around him he was going to "run in every primary from here to the end," scrapped his planned speech, spoke from the heart, and won that primary. From there he kept going until he could make history as President. He always felt that God was looking out for him, and he may have been right. In any case, I have never seen before or since a man with such political courage.

FRED BARNES

EXECUTIVE EDITOR, *THE WEEKLY STANDARD*

"I always found him to be much more astute and disciplined than he was given credit for."

For many years the White House correspondent for The New Republic, *Fred Barnes now writes about politics, public policy and the media as executive editor of the conservative journal* The Weekly Standard. *He is also a regular panelist on television's* The McLaughlin Group *and is frequently seen on CNN's* Crossfire.

What struck me about Ronald Reagan was how disciplined he was. He was much more astute and disciplined than he was given credit for. He didn't let out anything he didn't want let out. He was self-disciplined in a way that I, as a journalist, didn't find very helpful. But it was certainly a discipline that would help further his presidency.

I think of a lunch with him in 1986. Pat Buchanan, then the communications director at the White House, arranged for a couple of other journalists and me to join the President in that little room off the Oval Office. It was to be off-the-record. Of course, when you are a journalist, you say to yourself, "It's off-the-record but I'll still learn a lot of stuff and I can triangulate the information by getting other people to confirm it." So, when we went into lunch, I made sure I sat right next to the President. Don Regan, who was then chief of staff, was there, and, as I recall, so was Larry Speakes, then the press secretary.

We spent about an hour and a half over lunch. It was incredibly pleasant, but all I heard were Errol Flynn stories. The President answered our questions in general ways, but when it got down to specifics, he was really not going to divulge more than he would have in any other context. So, there wasn't anything to report that day, unless you wanted to use Errol Flynn stories.

I also remember a time in the late summer of 1984 when several of us in the press were invited to have a late afternoon chat with the President in the library, upstairs in the residential part of the White House. David Broder of *The Washington Post* and Bob Tyrrell of *The American Spectator* were there and two or three other journalists. This was after Walter Mondale had been nominated by the Democrats to challenge Reagan. We were eager to get Reagan to say something about Mondale. What did he think of this guy? You couldn't get it out of him. He went "off-the-record" this time, too, but it didn't make any difference. He was following that old adage attributed, I think, to Don Rumsfeld, "Nothing is really off-the-record in Washington, particularly when the President says it." So, here was a man with tremendous discipline—not exactly the popular image of him.

I recall a time in the 1980 campaign when there was a question whether Reagan was being accessible to the press. The fact was, he was accessible nearly all the time. We could come and ask him any questions we wanted to—but, he wouldn't tell you more than he wanted to. It was then I think I first recognized how disciplined he could be. In an intimate, pleasant setting such as a one-on-one or a small luncheon, he could turn the conversation any way you wanted to go—without leaking. He was certainly underestimated.

Another time—it was late 1987 or early '88—I had another interview with him. Howard Baker was then chief of staff. By then, Reagan had had cancer and had been operated on and he'd gone through the Iran-Contra business. He looked weary.

When Iran-Contra came up, the President said repeatedly that he did not believe it had been an arms-for-hostages deal. He hadn't intended it that way and it really wasn't. Tommy Griscom, then the communications director, and Marlin Fitzwater, the press secretary, sat there and winced. For months, his staff had been trying to get him to say it *was* arms-for-hostages and they finally did get him to say it—more than once—after *The Tower Report* came out. But he really didn't believe it. So, when he'd get one-on-one with a reporter, he would insist that it was not arms-for-hostages; it wasn't intended to be and shouldn't be construed that way. That was not the line his aides had been trying to put out, but no matter how hard they tried, they couldn't quash what the President believed to be true.

Reagan was very gracious in that interview. I brought in a photo of my mother with him taken back in the 1930s when he made a movie called *Sergeant Murphy*. Some of it was filmed at the Presidio in Monterey, California, where my grandfather was post commander. My mother was an extra in the film. Reagan remembered all about the movie—total recall of a film made fifty years before. He signed the photo.

There is one other thing I observed about Ronald Reagan over the years. Everyone said, "Well, he just had a good staff; the staff made him a success." If that were the case (and he did have good people working for him), then he would have been one of the first people in history to become one of the great leaders of his time by having about five different staffs—all absolutely brilliant and all pulling puppet strings absolutely perfectly! It defies reason that this could be the case. Even though he had good staff, they came, they went, and he was still a success. It was the same in campaigns. He was successful when John Sears was there, and he was successful when John Sears wasn't there. He succeeded because of his own abilities, his issues, and the way he connected with the people.

WILLARD "BARNEY" BARNETT

DRIVER, AIDE, FRIEND

"... the whole thing was ... just so much fun."

During the latter part of his career in the California Highway Patrol, "Barney" Barnett drove for two governors. First, Edmund G. "Pat" Brown; then, beginning in January 1967, Ronald Reagan. That month marked the start of a nearly thirty-year working relationship and friendship between two men of similar age. When Ronald Reagan left the governor's office in January 1975, Barney joined him in a private capacity, through presidential campaigns, the presidency, and afterward. Through it all, Barney was always there with a smile to welcome him home to southern California. Barney and Reagan worked side by side to turn the Reagans' Rancho del Cielo near Santa Barbara into a trim and comfortable, though simple, retreat.

Barney Barnett died on August 12, 1996, the same evening the Republican National Convention paid a warm tribute to his friend, "the boss."

We spent quite a lot of time at the ranch building fences. We used telephone poles and the President participated in putting just about every one of them in the ground. It was quite an experience. The poles were his idea because he had seen a fence built like this before. He, Dennis LeBlanc, and I got them all in the ground. I don't know how many miles we covered, but we put the fence completely around the ranch. We also worked together to fence the orchard and a little pasture of four or five acres for the horses in the summer.

In 1974, when the Reagans bought the property, there was just the little adobe cottage with a small trailer behind it. It wasn't really finished and there was a fence around the buildings to keep the cattle out. The President tore the whole front end off and had it redone. Then he and I did most of the work putting a new roof on the house. At various times, he'd take the lumber up there and we'd nail it in place, then put the roofing material over it. Sometimes the wind was so strong we could hardly stand on the roof. One time it blew large packages of roofing shingles right off just as we were about to use them. He'd go down the ladder, try to catch them, and bring them back up. By the time he did, another batch had blown off! We gave up for that day, but finished as soon as the weather improved.

President Reagan would never ask us to do anything he wouldn't do himself. We knew that if we didn't get it done, he'd do it, and we thought, that as governor of California or President of the United States, he shouldn't be working *that* hard.

But, the whole thing was . . . just so much fun.

BETSY BLOOMINGDALE
REAGAN FAMILY FRIEND

"Warm acts of kindness and 'lighting up the room.'
Even today he has that. He has been a man of his
time; it was meant to be."

*The Reagans' close friendship with Betsy Bloomingdale and her late husband,
Alfred, began long before Ronald Reagan's political career. They shared trips to
summer camp to visit their respective children, as well as countless intimate and
large social events.*

The wonderful sense of humor of this great man is one of
the memorable things about him. I remember the day of his
second inauguration, in January 1985. It was so cold the Inaugural
Parade had to be canceled. I went through the receiving line at
the White House wearing a fur hat made for the occasion. As I
came down the line, he looked at me, grinned, got that twinkle
in his eye, and said, "Tell me, how are things in Moscow?"

He gave me the nickname "Lady Bruce" during a visit to London in the 1970s. Walter Annenberg was our ambassador and he and his wife, Lee, had just refurbished the official residence, Winfield House, at their own expense. The Reagans and we were invited to a large dinner. Near the entrance was a seating chart for the dinner. Just beyond was a butler who announced the guests as they came into the main hall. Alfred and I were looking at the seating chart and he was reading off some names, looking for ours. As he scanned the chart, he read one listing, "Lady Bruce and Mr. Davis" just loud enough that the butler overheard us and thought we were telling *him* our names. So he announced us that way in a strong, formal voice. With that, Ronald Reagan laughed and, from that day to this, has always called me Lady Bruce. I had always wanted to be a "lady," so being Lady Bruce was wonderful!

His acts of kindness are legendary. Our eldest son has a ranch not far from the Reagans'. He had made a pond to catch rainwater and wanted to stock it with fish. When the President learned about it, he said to Geoffrey, "Why don't you come over and get some carp to fill your man-made lake?" When Geoff and his family went to Rancho del Cielo, the President got into the water and caught the fish for him. And this was at the height of his presidency! My son was so impressed, he's been a Republican ever since—and he was a onetime McGovern supporter!

Ronald Reagan always had a way of winning people over. One time—it was the same trip when we visited the Annenbergs—Alfred and I had been invited to a dinner party at Versailles by the curator and his wife. I mentioned to Florence Vanderkemp, the curator's wife, that the Reagans were coming to Paris. She knew Ronald Reagan was the governor of California and, in fact, was a supporter of his. She said they would be delighted to invite the Reagans. Most people in France, however, didn't have a clue as to who he was (or any other governors in the United States, for that matter).

The dinner was beautiful—candles, flowers, waiters in livery. There was a stunning guest list, including the Duke and Duchess of Windsor and a San Francisco woman who had been generous to France. She was to receive an award at the dinner from the French government for her help in preserving Versailles. After the presentation, they asked Governor Reagan to say a few words. He spoke beautifully, opening with a few words in French. Then he told the story of a film he had made in London (but about France). Everyone seemed to know the film's story. When he was finished, all these worldly French sophisticates were mad about him. He won them over completely. He was a very impressive man that night and, by the time they went home, everyone knew who the governor of California was.

Warm acts of kindness and the quality of "lighting up a room"—even today he has that. He has been a man of his time; it was meant to be.

EDMUND G. "JERRY" BROWN, JR.

GOVERNOR OF CALIFORNIA, 1975—82

"He was not just a guy across the table."

As governor of California, Ronald Reagan was both preceded and succeeded by a member of the Brown family. Edmund G. "Pat" Brown was trying for a third team when Ronald Reagan defeated him in 1966. Eight years later, in 1974, with Reagan declining to run for a third term (in pre-term-limit days), Pat's son Jerry was elected. Unlike his father, a bluff, hearty political traditionalist, Jerry, who had once trained to be a Jesuit priest, was iconoclastic. He didn't care for the trappings of office, preferring instead a spare, minimalist approach, although he was not anti-government per se. During the years when Reagan dominated the executive branch of California's government, Jerry Brown was elected twice as secretary of state. He went on to run for U.S. Senate in 1982, losing to Pete Wilson. In 1992, he ran strongly in the early primaries for the Democratic presidential nomination against Bill Clinton and a crowded field.

I remember sitting there in the governor's office with him, a couple of days after I had been elected to succeed him, eating a hamburger and a Coke. He had that Reagan smile. He was genial and told a few stories. Still, I have to say he was guarded. Having grown up around politicians, with my father being in public life, then getting into it myself, I felt Reagan had the quality of being somewhat apart. He was more distant, not aloof, and not distant in an unfriendly way. He was not just a guy across the table. He had a presence. He was not the hail-fellow-well-met kind of Irish politician. He had that quality of being able to tell a story, then smile and laugh, but he had the political traits in a way that did not make him seem like an old-time politician at all. There was a sort of magic there, and I could see it at work.

We didn't have a nuts-and-bolts conversation about the transition that day. I didn't see Ronald Reagan as a nuts-and-bolts kind of guy. There we were, representing opposing sides politically; two different philosophies that were brought together by the rules of politeness. It was very ceremonial, which is not my cup of tea or what I was used to at that point. He was definitely performing his ceremonial role as governor, and doing it quite well.

I think a great deal of the job is ceremonial. The way I look at it now, most politicians holding office think they are doing things, but it's all staffed-out. There is a certain momentum, depending on your political party's point of view, depending on what the need is, what's happening at the moment. There is a certain drift or inertia to public affairs, and the officeholder sort of drifts along with it. So his or her real role is ceremonial and symbolic. There may be a moment when the individual politician makes turns against the drift (such as when Reagan met with Gorbachev and said we should get rid of all nuclear weapons), but that's the exception.

Politicians generally are under the illusion that they are heavily engaged in some kind of thing when the reality is they are acting. They are acting to project an image. They deal in a world of symbols. Reagan, through his training as an actor and because of his temperament, could master that world in ways that most politicians could not. Most politicians don't really understand the nature of their work. It's not very often they go against the drift, the intertia. Most of the day-to-day stuff is very symbolic. That was one of the frustrations I found in being governor. At first, I took literally the nature of the material being presented at meetings, but I soon found that visiting delegations often were satisfied just being in the same room as the governor. There is something illusory about it, like a play. Then again, if that satisfies people, it has some value. Reagan seemed to understand all of that.

A few months after we had that transition meeting, we had the unveiling of Reagan's official gubernatorial painting in the capitol. The Reagans came up to Sacramento for it. It was a sentimental journey for him, I think, and a warm event.

BARBARA BUSH
FIRST LADY, 1989—93

"No wonder George loved him!"

Known for her energy and good humor, Barbara Bush has continued her work for charitable and humanitarian causes since leaving the White House in January 1993. Her primary cause is family literacy. She believes that if more people could read, write, and comprehend, many of society's problems would be closer to solutions. She is a board member of the Mayo Clinic Foundation and is active with Americares, the Leukemia Society of America, the Ronald McDonald House, and the Boys and Girls Clubs of America.

Mrs. Bush has authored three books: C. Fred's Story, Millie's Book *(the profits from which benefited the literacy cause), and* Barbara Bush: A Memoir.

Born Barbara Pierce, she was reared in Rye, New York. She and George Bush were married on January 6, 1945, and together preside over a large family consisting of four sons, one daughter, four daughters-in-law, one son-in-law, and fourteen grandchildren.

Ronald Reagan is innately polite—a real gentleman. I remember once—in the beginning of the administration—the chief of protocol, Lee Annenberg, briefed us before an event. "Mr. President, you and Mrs. Reagan will go first, and then Vice President and Mrs. Bush will follow," she said. When we got to the door, it opened and President Reagan stepped back and said, "After you, Barbara. Ladies first." It's a small story, but it typifies his kindness.

I never heard anyone say that Ronald Reagan was anything but polite. He spoke to everyone with the same gentleness—waiters, presidents, security guards—whomever. He was always a gentleman—no wonder George loved him!

GEORGE BUSH
FORTY-FIRST PRESIDENT OF THE UNITED STATES

"Ronald Reagan's most important contributions to the nation were his decency, his sense of honor, and the deep feeling he conveyed to the entire world that America is the greatest country on the face of the earth."

When he was sworn in as President of the United States on January 20, 1989, succeeding Ronald Reagan, George Bush was the first sitting Vice President to ascend to the presidency since Martin Van Buren in 1837.

After a successful business career in Texas, he began a public service career in 1966, being elected to the House of Representatives from Texas's Seventh Congressional District. He served two terms, then began a series of senior-level government appointments. He was U.S. ambassador to the United Nations (1971), chairman of the Republican National Committee (1973), chief of the U.S. Liaison Office in China (1974), and director of the Central Intelligence Agency. In 1980, he was Ronald Reagan's principal rival for the Republican presidential nomination.

He joined the ticket at the Republican convention in Detroit, then served eight years as Vice President.

As Vice President, my working relationship with President Reagan was confidential and close. I tried to be supportive of him in every way. If I had a disagreement on policy, I always felt free to tell him about that difference in private. I think he knew I would not go public or try to feather my own nest. I could no more have betrayed that trust than flown to the moon. He was too good a man to ever have to worry about his Vice President's loyalty.

Kindness has always been a great characteristic of his. There are countless examples of his many kindnesses to the people around him. He never walked by a doorman or elevator operator or groundskeeper at the White House without acknowledging that person and making them feel warm and welcome.

Ronald Reagan has always been a great teller of jokes, too. At our private weekly luncheons, each of us would run out our latest jokes. Even if he repeated a joke, he told it so well that you couldn't help but laugh all over again.

One small recollection that still amuses me had to do with the fact that he used to feed the squirrels on the White House grounds. I told him that our dogs, Millie and Ranger, had gotten into the habit of chasing squirrels and, if they caught them, did them in. Just before I became President, President Reagan had a sign made for the squirrels that he put just outside the Oval Office. It read, "Beware of dogs."

All in all, I think Ronald Reagan's most important contributions to the nation were his decency, his sense of honor, and the deep feeling he conveyed to the entire world that America is the greatest country on the face of the earth.

LOU CANNON
REPORTER, *THE WASHINGTON POST*

"The hidden strength of this man is his consistent human dimension."

As a reporter, Lou Cannon probably covered Ronald Reagan longer and more comprehensively than any other journalist. He covered Governor Reagan, presidential candidate Reagan, and President Reagan for The Washington Post. *His early career was on newspapers in Nevada and California, covering sports, crime, and local government before moving to the Sacramento bureau of the* San Jose Mercury-News *in the mid-1960s. He is the author of several books, including* President Reagan: The Role of a Lifetime.

It was in the fall of 1965 when I first met Ronald Reagan and covered him. I was with the *San Jose Mercury-News* at that time. He was going around California, trying to show that he was more than an actor. He would talk for just a few minutes, then throw it open to questions.

One day he was going to talk to a press group in Sacramento and one of my editors suggested I go over and hear him. It wasn't even a formal assignment; it was just, "You might be interested in hearing him." I was and I went. He handled the questions well enough, but two other things I noticed in particular were that he liked reporters and they seemed to like him, and that he was a real celebrity. They crowded around him afterward. That's not what reporters usually did.

Those were the days when the Democrats were sure that Governor Pat Brown could win a third term—if only the Republicans would nominate Reagan. I said to my editor, "I don't understand why anyone would want to run against this guy." "Why not?" he asked. "Well, he's a friendly person and people like him and I don't think that's what people want to run against." Long before my editor died, this story had taken on a mythical quality; that I had said Reagan was going to run for President!

Sometimes first impressions can be misleading, but that first impression of Ronald Reagan was one of the more valid ones I have had of any person in public life. His unremitting friendliness—he really liked people and they liked him—was one of his assets, his better qualities. His charm was genuine.

Another thing I noticed was that he talked in the vernacular. He talked to people the way they talked to him. He wasn't rhetorical at all. That was a great quality of his and he never lost it when he became President. He had the ability to talk to people at whatever their level without patronizing them.

The other thing I noticed about him early on was that he had a really good sense of humor. He joked constantly with his aides and with us in the press corps. He'd tell us stories about the movie business, which we all liked. I recall one time, one of the reporters brought him a picture of Reagan with the chimpanzee from the movie *Bedtime for Bonzo*. Reagan signed it and wrote, "I'm the one with the watch."

During 1968, I was writing a book about Reagan and Jesse Unruh, who was then the speaker of the assembly. I arranged to travel with him in 1968 when he made an extraordinary number of speeches for Republican candidates all over the country. I was with him for long periods of time and saw that his wit was not the product of his staff, but was natural. He joked and kidded and had comebacks. He had good lines that were impromptu, not rehearsed.

When you are regularly covering a person as I did Reagan and you are doing it in the pressure cooker of *The Washington Post*, there are times you will write things that may be harmful to the candidate—and all the staff get really angry with you. The interesting thing about Reagan was that I've been in situations where he denounced me on national television about something I wrote, but it wasn't personal with him. He understood I was doing my job. When he was in the White House, I remember he would yap about Sam Donaldson, but then say that Sam had a job to do. He never took criticism personally.

The only time I remember him being angry was when a columnist wrote a snide and unfair column about Nancy. He was really upset. It was in Louisiana in the 1980 presidential campaign. He wanted to talk about it when I went to interview him. He wanted to know what I thought about it. The same day, there were four or five articles in the papers eviscerating him, but that didn't bother him. What really bothered him was that someone would write in such an unfair way about his wife.

I think the root of the strength of this man is his consistent human dimension. He was a star, a celebrity, a big shot—but he never acted that way. He didn't put on airs. He knew who he was and stayed that way all his life.

When my mother died, it hit me hard. I didn't expect this to happen because she had been very ill and we expected it, but it was still a big shock. I said to him, "Mr. President, I thought I was prepared for this." He said, "You're never prepared for the death of your mother." This struck me as one of the kindest things anyone had ever said to me.

Over the years, I wrote about him round and square, this way and that way. Some of his policies I thought were terrific and some I thought were not, but all of that didn't matter at the end. Policies change, people come and go, but on the human level as a man, he was just fine. He treated me and others decently. That meant more to me than what he had done as President or politician. People felt he cared about them and had their interest at heart.

A lot of the old politicians and people who had been his adversaries thought highly of him, too. Pat Brown called on him when he came to Washington. Willie Brown, the longtime speaker of the California assembly (and now mayor of San Francisco), Tip O'Neill, and others with very different political views from his came to like him as a person.

In a campaign, he gave as good as he got, but he was never vicious about an opponent. He was not out to destroy anyone. He might vehemently attack someone's policy or proposal, but not the person. That's a quality we could use a lot more of.

GEORGE CHRISTOPHER

FORMER MAYOR OF SAN FRANCISCO;
1966 POLITICAL OPPONENT

"In retrospect, I believe it benefited the country when
I lost the governorship to him because, had I won, he
would not have become President."

*Twice elected mayor of San Francisco, George Christopher is a native of that city
and received his entire high school and college education at night school, while
holding down a daytime job. He later founded a successful dairy products business
before entering politics. During his terms as mayor, President Eisenhower praised
him as "an exceptionally talented administrator." In 1981, he was a U.S. delegate
to the United Nations. He holds decorations for fostering international goodwill
from a number of countries. Here he recalls the 1966 Republican primary for
California's governorship, in which he and Ronald Reagan were rivals.*

My mind races back to 1966, about two years after I had
retired as an eight-year mayor of San Francisco. A contingent of

well-wishers was urging me to run for governor of California and, after many days of deliberation, I decided it was well worth the effort.

I had heard of Ronald Reagan, of course, but I believed what so many people were saying, that "an actor" couldn't win the Republican primary over a businessman-politician. Well, the "actor" turned out to be a superb politician, who knew how to persuade the vast audiences we were soon addressing.

In Orange County one day, during the question-and-answer period, we were both asked how we would administer the then-huge state budget of $4.5 billion. Mr. Reagan replied that any state, like any business, could cut its budget by 10 percent. He received an ovation. My reply was, "The budget can only be reduced by freezing hiring and deleting jobs by attrition." In all my years in politics, I received from this audience the all-time high for boos, which are still ringing in my ears! I learned a good lesson that day. I was up against a master communicator who, in his own quiet but eloquent way, always presented a very convincing case.

Someone said to me, "Yes, but he reads everything from those four-by-six-inch cards." My response was, "Let's get the fellows who prepare those cards!" The fact was that he prepared most of them and nobody else could read them and convey the same conviction or care for our state's and nation's objectives as he did. And he did it in a very simple, dignified, unassuming way.

There was no rancor when I lost the primary election to him. While I lost the nomination to Ronald Reagan at a time when the polls showed me running ahead of Governor Pat Brown, I am consoled that, as a result of Reagan's victory over me, his service as governor catapulted him to the presidency. In retrospect, I believe it benefited the country that I lost the governorship to him because, had I won, he would not have become President.

Over the years, I have had many letters from him, especially from the days when I formed a national committee to support his election to the presidency. I traveled to many eastern cities, organized groups, and raised money for his campaign—and always received a cordial letter of thanks for my efforts. Later, he appointed me as an alternate delegate to the United Nations, an assignment I enjoyed very much.

Ronald Reagan rendered great service to America, because he knew how to choose able, intelligent, and dedicated personnel and advisers who steered our country onto a constructive course.

TONY COELHO
FORMER DEMOCRATIC (MAJORITY) WHIP,
U.S. HOUSE OF REPRESENTATIVES

"Does the President know what you've said?"

Tony Coelho was first elected to Congress from California's San Joaquin Valley in 1978. From 1981 to 1987, he was chairman of the Democratic Congressional Campaign Committee, then joined the House leadership as majority whip, the third-ranking position. He resigned his seat in 1989 and joined Wertheim Schroder and Company, a New York investment banking firm, where he was managing director until 1995, when he founded the firm he now heads, Coelho Associates. Active in civic affairs, he was appointed chairman of the President's Committee on Employment of People with Disabilities in 1994 and, in 1996, commissioner general of the U.S. delegation to Expo '98, the next world's fair, to be held in Lisbon, Portugal.

Ronald Reagan believed a few things and he really stood for them. He was "presidential." He didn't get down in the gutter.

Indeed, he would let people accuse him of anything. We did, but these things never got a response. No doubt he didn't like a lot of the things that were said about him by opponents, but for the most part he did not take them personally.

One time, before the State of the Union speech, he came to the Speaker's office—by tradition—to meet with leaders of both parties. We would chat for a few minutes, then all be escorted into the House chamber. The first time I participated in this ceremony was January 1987. I had just finished six years as chairman of the Democratic House Campaign Committee and had been beating up on Reagan every chance I got. As I walked into the room, Reagan was talking with someone, so I stood, waiting to shake his hand, which was the protocol. As I waited, Senator Alan Simpson walked up and said to me, "Does the President know who you are and what you've said about him?" I thought he said this loud enough for everyone to hear, but I don't know if Reagan heard it or not. If he did, he didn't let on. He was very gracious as we met and later sent me an autographed photo.

Every other week, the House and Senate leaders got together with the President. There were fifteen to twenty people around the Cabinet table in the White House. When I became majority whip, I was automatically included. At my first meeting, I was all eyes and ears, trying to pick up everything that was going on. The President came in and we all stood up. He sat down, pulled out a card, and went over the agenda. I soon learned that those meetings lasted just one hour, no more, no less. If the agenda—which he had written out on cards—wasn't completed at the end of the hour, he would excuse himself and leave. If it was finished short of an hour, he would fill the rest of the time with jokes (and he tells a good one).

During 1987, we had many such meetings with the President and others in the White House over the troubles in Central America. I was majority whip at the time. We finally negotiated a compromise with the White House, but neither side fully trusted the other. At one of these meetings it was decided that if some difficulty arose, Colin Powell would be the point man for the White House and I would be for the congressional majority.

The idea was that we would talk things over and try to keep the situation calm. In Washington, it's not so much the facts but the perception that counts and, in this area, Reagan was very protective of his interests. In some of our White House meetings on various subjects, I did not feel he was fully engaged or interested in what was being discussed; but on this issue of Central America he definitely was.

SAM DONALDSON
WHITE HOUSE CORRESPONDENT, ABC NEWS

"His most outstanding leadership quality was that you knew where he stood."

With ABC News since 1967, Sam Donaldson is one the nation's best-known television journalists. He is coanchor of PrimeTime Live *and* This Week. *(The latter, as* This Week with David Brinkley, *included him as a panelist from its inception in 1981 until David Brinkley's retirement in 1996.) He was ABC's chief White House correspondent from 1979 to 1989, spanning all eight of the Reagan years. A native of Texas, he began his broadcasting career at KRLD-TV in Dallas in 1959, then moved to WTOP-TV in Washington. His autobiography,* Hold On, Mr. President!, *was published in 1987.*

Among those of us who have covered him, Ronald Reagan is still a fascinating object of conversation. I can't imagine the people covering Bill Clinton spending the time talking about him ten years later as they do Reagan.

I was not a social friend of his; reporters are not with office-holders. But, for me, Reagan was like radar. If those in the media around him came to public attention or prominence, it was primarily a reflection of being in his orbit. It was a reflection of his energy rather than our own. His energy would paint you the way a radar screen paints you.

Reagan understood the press. I interviewed him three or four times when he was governor of California, but I really didn't get to know him until he was in the White House. He understood what we were doing and why we were doing it. People would comment that even though I asked sharp questions, he and I always seemed to be smiling. I don't think he liked criticism any more than other Presidents or public figures like it, but he was secure enough that it rolled off his back more than I've seen it roll off other Presidents' backs.

In my case, I think he knew—even though some of his partisans didn't—that I bore him no ill will. (Somewhere in my attic I have bushels of letters from his fans in the 1980s telling me what a vicious mad dog I was and that I hated him. Far from it.) When I asked him questions, I thought they were legitimate questions of public interest and, on occasion, of personal interest. People are interested in Presidents' lives and, besides, Reagan is also an actor. I use that word in the best sense, not in disparagement. After all, why shouldn't he be a good actor? That was his whole life and training. There's a bit of ham in me, I suppose, and I think one ham recognizes another.

One time, he was at the Berlin Wall at Checkpoint Charlie, standing on one side of the line that marked the no-man's-land between West and East Berlin. He was standing on the Western side and I hollered, "Mr. President, watch out that you don't get captured by those dirty commies!" So, he lifted his right leg and got that mischievous smile on his face and danced his leg in the air, over the line.

That great sense of humor was always with him, but I must

say that when Ronald Reagan walked into a room, you knew the President of the United States was present. In recent times, I have been to receptions where you are standing and talking to people and realize that the guy who is sort of gliding by is Bill Clinton. Nobody said he had come in, nobody announced him, and you say to yourself, "I don't want the guy next door to be President, I just want him over on Saturday night." When Carter was President, at first he tried pretending to be just one of the guys, but soon realized that it was a serious mistake.

As to Reagan's mind, I always thought he had a good one. He was not, as some of his detractors thought, putty in the hands of those around him. It's true, however, that sometimes he chose not to use his mind on a subject many thought the President should be intimately connected with. On the other hand, when he was engaged on a subject, it was awesome the way he focused on it.

One time, we were leaving the Rose Garden and we were shouting questions at him. Although he's hard of hearing, he'd often hear things he wanted to hear and, with the other questions, say, "What? What?" On this day, he clearly didn't want to answer any more serious questions as he was going up the steps into the White House. I called out, congratulating him on the new suit he was wearing (I didn't think I had seen it before). He was out of camera range and said, "No, Sam, this suit's about four years old." I went back to my cubicle in the press room and five minutes later I got a call from the President. "Yes, Mr. President," I said. He said, "I misinformed you when I left to go back to the Oval Office. I looked at the label in the suit and realized where I bought it and it came back to me that the suit wasn't four years old, but five." It bowled me over. One part of me said, "Is that all the President of the United States has to do?" But the other part realized what a kind and genuine human being he was. Bill Plante (of CBS) had an appendix operation and the President called him at the hospital. When I was to be married to Jan Smith, he called me in Kansas City, where we were having an engagement party. He said, "Sam, you know what the song says: It's better the second time around." I didn't have the heart to tell him it was the third time for me and just said, "Yes, sir."

When he was up at his ranch, the hardest decision the reporters had to make was where to go for dinner. There was no real news, just the routine "ranch report" every day. One night, I was talking live with Barbara Walters on *20/20* and she asked me what was going on. I said, "Nothing much. We have the ranch report here and, once again, he chopped wood and cleared brush. I suspect that just before he gets there, they haul up truckloads of brush and wood for him to chop because, if he chopped as much as they say he does, there wouldn't be any trees left on the ranch."

Well, Reagan was watching, and the next day, I'm told, he called his ranch foreman and said he wanted all the brush he had cleared over the last week or ten days piled up in one place by the house. They did, and he had a photographer take pictures of it from all angles. He sent me one of the photos, on which he had written, "Dear Sam, Here's the proof I chopped it all with my own little hatchet." Talk about focus!

In matters of public policy, he set the tone. Everyone knew what he wanted to accomplish. Take the Iran-Contra issue. Many people, including myself, believed that he didn't know what Oliver North was doing and that he was quite capable of forgetting the details of what was said about the Israelis at certain times. I think if he had known what North was up to, he would not have condoned it. He was too honest and honorable to support such things.

Sometimes, with his news conference answers, I found myself thinking, "That's too candid." One time, I stood up and said, "Mr. President, Jesse Helms is saying on the floor of the Senate that Martin Luther King, Jr., was a Communist sympathizer. Do you agree?" He said, "Well, we'll know in thirty-five years, won't we?" (That was when the King papers were to be unsealed.) I was told later that his staff had expected that question and that he had given that very answer to it in the prep session before the news conference. His staff thought he was only kidding and were shocked when he used it because it certainly wasn't the "political" thing to say. This was one time when relying on his instincts wasn't the right thing to do. Usually, though, his political instincts, when he applied them, were often better than those of the people around him. And, when he put his mind to an issue and actually took over, you'd get a pretty good solution to the problem, based on his own ideology. If he just left it to others, as was sometimes the case in his second term, it was arms to the Ayatollah, and so forth.

I don't think we've ever had a President who used the "bully pulpit" better than he did. He was its master. I've often said to others that his most outstanding leadership quality was that you knew where he stood on a matter. You didn't have to agree with him. Where I had disagreements with him, it was about policies I thought were wrong, but I sure knew what they were. I never had to figure out what kind of speech he'd give tomorrow or worry that he'd change his mind from the views he expressed today.

He had the showman's sense of knowing when he would be over-exposed, so he never was. But, I recall a time when he went the other way—six months between news conferences. I give Bush—and Clinton, too—credit for talking more to the press themselves than Reagan did. On the other hand, there can be too much of a good thing. There must be a happy medium.

I subscribe to that well-known theory that the sons of alcoholic fathers often retreat into a world of fantasy, or at least one more ideal than real. I think this phenomenon affected Reagan. I don't want to argue that point too strongly, but it was a source of his charm and, perhaps, his political strength. He would often see things as better than they were. For instance, when we were in what was called the Paul Volcker Recession, he said at one news conference, "You know, people are saying they can't find jobs and unemployment is high. But, I looked in *The Washington Post* last Sunday and there were forty-four pages of want ads." I said, respectfully, "Yes, sir, but they were for computer operators; for people with skills." I think he saw the situation as one where anyone who wanted a job could find one, but that was not really the case.

There was some kind of disconnect between the effects of some of his policy positions and his personal generosity. One time when he saw an item in the newspaper about a boy who needed a kidney transplant, he sent the family $1,000 of his own money, without a word to anyone. It would never have been known had the family not publicly expressed its gratitude. In personal instances of this sort, he had the warmest heart of anyone I knew. But, as I recall, the year he sent the money to that family, he signed a bill that cut funding for the National Institutes of Health for recipients of organ transplants. I'll bet dollars to doughnuts he didn't know that his signature would do that, but he should have known. Had he known, I think, he would have personalized it. Every time he did, he came out on the right side of the issue.

One time, early on, he was talking about how human rights would be a cornerstone of his policy. It was in response to a question about dealing with other nations. His staff was horrified because they thought it made him sound like Jimmy Carter and part of the plan was to pull back from Carter policy to a more realistic, national-interest-type foreign policy. But, he didn't have any script; it was just Ronald Reagan talking. The next day, we had clarification from Jim Baker and others along the lines of "Of course we're interested in human rights; however . . ."

When I get together with other political reporters who have been around since the 1960s, we talk some about Kennedy and Goldwater, but it is still Ronald Reagan we talk about most. He is the center, the force. Kennedy is in a special niche (despite that awful word "Camelot"), but Reagan is the most dynamic President I have seen. The one with the most force; the biggest radar of the lot.

I was always a fan of Nancy Reagan's, too. I liked her. I had no problem with her fierce dedication to her husband's political and physical safety. My wife is sort of that way, and I think it's terrific. The Reagans clearly love each other and, when all is said and done, that's what counts most.

KENNETH DUBERSTEIN
PRESIDENTIAL CHIEF OF STAFF, 1988

"He threw the ball up in the air a foot or two to dramatize the idea."

Ken Duberstein served as chief of staff for Ronald Reagan's last year in office, after serving as deputy chief of staff for the year previous. In President Reagan's first term, he had been assistant to the President for legislative affairs. He also served in the Ford and Nixon administrations. Considered a particularly astute observer of the ways of Washington, he now heads his own planning and consulting company that gives clients strategic advice. He also serves on the boards of several corporations and civic organizations.

At the 1987 summit with Gorbachev in Washington, the first session was held in the Cabinet Room. There were too many people there. Gorbachev dominated the session. The President was somewhat disconcerted. That night at the state dinner he gave a toast that recaptured some of the initiative, but he was worried about how the next morning would unfold. George Shultz, Frank Carlucci, Howard Baker, and I worked on talking points for him. The President's plan was to lead off for fifteen minutes, laying down his thoughts and agenda. We also decided to move the meeting to the Oval Office rather than have thirty or forty people sitting around the Cabinet Room.

That first night, at the state dinner, Maureen Reagan brought a baseball for Joe DiMaggio—who was there—to autograph. The next morning, the President told us about it. I suggested that, at the beginning of the session, he take Gorbachev into the President's study, off the Oval Office, for a heart-to-heart talk, with only translators there. He did that as soon as Gorbachev arrived. In the study, he showed Gorbachev the baseball and explained an American expression. He said, "Mr. President, do you want to play ball, or do you want to be stuck in ideological differences?" He threw the ball up in the air a foot or two to dramatize the idea. The President later told us that Gorbachev said, "Let's play ball." They returned to the Oval Office where Reagan led with his fifteen-minute agenda remarks. He made it clear what terms he would accept. It turned around the summit. It put the President on top again.

Speaking of baseball, he enjoyed telling anecdotes about broadcasting Chicago Cubs baseball games when he was at radio station WHO in Des Moines. So, I asked him early in 1988, "How would you like to go to Wrigley Field this season and visit the broadcasting booth?" I reminded him of his call to Harry Carey, the Cubs' announcer, when he'd learned that Carey was recovering from a heart attack. "I think Harry Carey would love to have you join him in the broadcast booth," I said. "I'd really like to do that if you think they'd like me to," was his reply. We started looking over his schedule for opportunities. During the last week of the baseball season, he was to do an event for George Bush's presidential campaign on the South Side of Chicago. At the end of this event, we took a small motorcade to Wrigley Field, notifying Harry Carey about an hour in advance that the President would be there (Reagan didn't want to create a fuss). He warmed up in the Cubs' locker room, because he would throw out the first pitch. Some of the Cubs watched as he practiced. He was having a hard time getting the ball over an imaginary home plate. I said, "You've got to get it a little more over the plate, Mr. President." He said, with a big smile, "No, as long as I'm throwing them far to the right, they're okay." He went out to the mound and threw the opening pitch right over the plate. Then he went up to the broadcasting booth and Harry Carey welcomed him to the simultaneous radio-television broadcast. The President said, "Well, in a few months I'm going to be out of a job and looking for a new one, so I thought I'd start by auditioning here." He called the plays for an inning and a half. CNN broke into their regular program to cover the President broadcasting the game. It was on the network news that evening and in most newspapers the next day. He was having such a good time, he didn't want to leave. And, the polling done that weekend showed George Bush up six points in Illinois!

In the Oval Office, he often made phone calls to members of Congress, not just to lobby them, but to find out what was going on in their districts. He would say, "I'm not looking for your vote for anything. I just want to know what happened at your last town meeting. What are people thinking or talking about?" That flattered the congressman or congresswoman and gave the President contact with the mood of the country.

People used to say to me that I was very fortunate in his first term, when I was his chief congressional liaison, that I had the best lobbyist in the world at my disposal, the President of the United States. I told him that one day and he said, "No, Ken, I'm the second best. 'First best' are the people back home who vote, because if I can connect with them, they will make sure their members of Congress vote the way I want them to." That was one of the secrets of his success.

He had some good luck, too. When he was recovering back at the White House from the 1981 assassination attempt, we were looking for members of Congress who would help us break the dam on his budget plan, and not just Southern "Boll Weevil" Democrats. He had a list of members to call who we thought might be persuaded to join him. One of them happened to be on a congressional delegation trip to Australia with Tip O'Neill. I didn't realize he had gone on the trip. The White House operator found him in Australia at what was 3:00 A.M. there. The next morning, the President said to me, "I got him on the phone. He was groggy and I asked him, 'What time is it?' He said, 'It's three o'clock in the morning and I'm in Australia.' All I felt like saying at that point was, 'This is Jimmy Carter. Good-bye.' " He did add that he asked the congressman to come to the Oval Office for a visit about the budget on his return.

At about the same time, he called a Democratic congressman from Pennsylvania who had indicated he might be interested in helping us on the budget, but wasn't quite ready to commit. The White House operator located this congressman at a live radio call-in show in his district. This was a bit of Reagan luck. The next voice you heard on the radio was that of Ronald Reagan asking this congressman for his vote on the first budget resolution (known as Gramm-Latta). The congressman, a bit flustered, committed himself on the spot—and on the air. It was the first time since the assassination attempt that the American people had heard Ronald Reagan's voice. The story led all three networks that night. And, it was the first time he had broken through with northern and midwestern Democrats on that first budget vote. Sixty-three Democrats ended up voting for his position.

On January 29, 1989, following George Bush's inauguration as President, the helicopter carrying the Reagans lifted off from the east front of the Capitol. There were six or seven of us aboard. The helicopter took what has become a ceremonial swing around Washington for each departing President. As it circled the White House, Reagan looked out the window. He took Nancy's hand and said, "Look, dear, there's our little bungalow." Nancy had a tear in her eye; we all did.

LEE EDWARDS
EDITOR, AUTHOR

"I thought, 'President,' and wrote it in my note-book."

Senior editor of The World and I *magazine, Lee Edwards is also an adjunct assistant professor at at the Catholic University of America, a senior fellow at the Heritage Foundation and president of the Victims of Communism Memorial Foundation. In addition to his* Ronald Reagan: A Political Biography, *published in 1967 and again in 1981, he is the author of six books and numerous articles. In 1985, he was a fellow at the Institute of Politics, John F. Kennedy School of Government at Harvard University.*

The first year Ronald Reagan was governor of California, 1967, I became his first biographer. The book covered his life up to the first few months of his governorship, so it included some of his goals in office. In it, I also related the story of his having his inauguration take place at one minute after midnight so that his predecessor, Pat Brown, wouldn't have an extra twelve hours or so in which to grant more pardons.

I spent a lot of time with him in the course of working on that book, and it is still vivid in my mind after so many years. In the summer of 1965, I was working on a magazine article about him and I wrote to him and asked for an appointment. It would be my first meeting with him, although I had known about him since 1964 when I had been working on the Barry Goldwater presidential campaign and Reagan gave that famous speech.

My wife joined me for the trip to California and we spent two days traveling around with Ronald Reagan. He was traveling about the state, meeting with people, to ascertain if they wanted him to run for governor. At that point, he wasn't sure, so he was conducting a trial run, so to speak. Although Anne and I were comparatively young, we had already been around a number of major political figures, which is why I wanted to see him up close. During those two days, we traveled in the car with him. I had a tape recorder with me and would ask questions as we drove about southern California.

The first night, when we got back to where we were staying, I asked Anne, who had been head of the Young Women's Republican Club in New York City and had known Nelson Rockefeller, John Lindsay, and Jacob Javits, if Ronald Reagan really had *it*. She was excited and exclaimed, "Yes, he definitely has *it*."

The next day, late in the afternoon, after traveling about and meeting groups, he asked if we would like to come up to their home in Pacific Palisades for some iced tea. We sat in the living room while he excused himself to go to the kitchen to make the iced tea with Nancy. While he was out of the room, I went over to the library because the rap on him at the time was that he wasn't very smart, didn't read, was superficial, and wasn't much of an ideas man. The room was lined with bookcases filled with books. Clearly, all had been read, because, as I glanced through a number of them, I found dog-ears and bookmarks. Most of the books were on economics, history, and politics. I said to myself,

"If this man is this serious about what he stands for and is so charismatic that the crowds virtually glow when he is near them, then he is bound for big things nationally." I thought, "President," and wrote it in my notebook.

For the Reagan biography, one of the people I interviewed was his escort executive at General Electric, Earl Dunckel. I asked him what it was like to be with Ronald Reagan on those long train trips, visiting GE plants (Reagan had it written into his contract that he would not be required to fly). What would he do on those trips to, say, New York and Texas? I asked. Dunckel said, "He would read newspapers, magazines, and books and be making notes all the time. He'd scribble on cards; he'd underline articles." Thus began a habit he continued throughout his career in public life.

Over the years, as I followed his progress, I interviewed him from time to time. In 1976, when I was editor of *Conservative Digest,* we put him on the cover during the Republican convention in Kansas City. I interviewed him in his office in Los Angeles for that article. In the course of it, something happened that I'll never forget. I had my list of questions and tape recorder. It was just Ronald Reagan and me, sitting a few feet apart on a sofa, with the coffee table in front of us. I was interviewing him when, all of a sudden about halfway through, I came to with a start. I realized I was not daydreaming, I was actually mesmerized by his voice. I can't put it any other way: I was mesmerized by his voice and personality. I realized the tape recorder had been running all the time. It was an extraordinary demonstration of his voice reaching out and enveloping his listener. He could do it one-on-one or to thousands in an auditorium. It was a rare quality.

When he was running for President in 1980, I decided to revise and edit my biography of him. I brought it up to date to about the time John Hinckley tried to assassinate him in March 1981. When the book was printed in late 1981, I arranged to present a copy to President Reagan. In order to promote sales, the publisher had put a bright yellow banner across the cover, screaming that this was "complete through the assassination attempt." That was not in the greatest taste, but it did get attention. I presented the book to him in the Oval Office and he had this wonderful smile. While the photographers were snapping pictures, I could see he was looking down at the book, thinking of something to say. Finally, he looked up at me, smiling, and said, "Lee, I'm sorry I messed up your ending." It was that wonderful Reagan wit at work. I burst out laughing.

M. STANTON EVANS
TEACHER, PUBLISHER, COMMENTATOR, EDITOR,
CONSERVATIVE ACTIVIST

"He isn't radical at all."

Stan Evans is a man of multiple talents. He served as editor of the Indianapolis News *from 1960 to 1974; has been a commentator on CBS radio and television networks, a nationally syndicated columnist from 1973 to 1985, visiting professor of journalism, publisher of* Consumer's Research *magazine; and is today director of the National Journalism Center in Washington, D.C. He has also served as chairman of the American Conservative Union and is the author of six books, including* The Future of Conservatism.

My first recollection of having any personal contact with Ronald Reagan was about 1962. Our local chamber of commerce in Indianapolis was staging a series of lectures they were calling the Voice of Freedom Series. They were very interested in getting Mr. Reagan to be one of the guest speakers. I was then editor of the local newspaper and they thought I might have more success in getting through to him, although I did not know him.

I can't remember how we got his phone number, but we did and I got through to him. I recall vividly how friendly and accessible he was to me, a stranger calling. We chatted, not only about the speaking engagement (I think he accepted), but also about the movies. By coincidence, the night before I had seen on television *The Winning Team,* a film about the baseball great Grover Cleveland Alexander, in which Reagan had starred. I mentioned it to him, and we got into a conversation about it. I'm a baseball fan and, watching the film, I recognized some of the real ballplayers who had played the nineteenth-century players in the film. A lot of them were ex-Chicago Cubs. One was Peanuts Lowry, third baseman for the Cubs. So Reagan and I got to discussing the Cubs and his broadcasting of their games. It was a wonderfully engaging conversation. He was, first of all, a nice guy. I don't think at that time I had ever heard him deliver an address. I knew that he had been out speaking for General Electric and I had seen him on television as well as in the movies. I don't think I had ever heard anything political from him. So, my initial impression was not in the political framework at all; rather, that he was just a very nice man. And that, of course, has never changed.

Then I remember being awed by his marvelous speech for Senator Goldwater toward the end of the 1964 presidential campaign. I don't think I had any other contact with Ronald Reagan between 1962 and the Goldwater speech. Then he ran for governor and won. Not long after he was inaugurated in 1967, I went to California for some other purpose, but also asked for and got an appointment with him. I wanted to find out all about his plans as governor. We had a good conversation and I wrote some articles from it. I soon became an enthusiast for him to become President. In 1968, of course, it was problematic because he had just been sworn in as governor, so to run for President was a difficult thing to do. Nevertheless, I thought he had every quality that was needed. In terms of the progression of Republican politics, he seemed to represent the next stage (if you look at Goldwater as being a more modern version of Robert Taft). Senator Goldwater had some negatives, which the liberal media took pains to exaggerate. Reagan had a gift, an art for diffusing negatives and for presenting things in a way that could not be made to frighten people (although the opposition tried).

In that summer of 1967, I wrote a book, *The Future of Conservatism,* that came out the next spring. In it, I wrote that he had all the attributes that were needed in a President, and I advocated that he run. My preference was for Reagan rather than Nixon, but a number of my conservative friends were signing on for Nixon early in 1968, including Goldwater himself, and Senators Strom Thurmond and John Tower. The book enjoyed modest success, and I feel pretty good that what I had advocated all came to pass, though years later. In 1968, when Reagan's friends mounted that brief, abortive nomination effort at the convention in Miami Beach, I played a small role by contributing to a small book titled *Reasons for Reagan* that circulated among enthusiasts for him.

Although I was not well-acquainted personally with Reagan in those days, just by thinking analytically and observing the state of the country, I concluded that he had the abilities to go all the way. The so-called pragmatists in the Republican party—who always want a winner, above all else—showed their obtuseness when it came to Reagan. They were incapable of recognizing a winner when they had one. They did everything they could to prevent him from getting the nomination.

Through his gubernatorial years, I watched him from afar. Our Indiana governor, Ed Whitcomb, to a considerable degree modeled his programs after Reagan's. Toward the end of Reagan's second term, thoughts of the presidency again began to stir and I visited California several times to meet with those around him. Nixon was still in the White House. I remember discussions on what posture Reagan should assume toward the Nixon issue and how difficult it was for him.

Then, in early 1975, there were debates among many conservative activists about whether he should run in the Republican party or outside of it. Bill Rusher wrote a book advocating the new-party idea and Jeff Bell, inside the Reagan camp, was for it. At the time, I had the feeling he had a better chance at the presidency from outside the GOP. But he decided to stay inside, and that was that. He isn't radical at all. He's a straight-ahead type guy.

Then he announced his intention to seek the 1976 Republican presidential nomination. I did get involved at this point. I was chairman of the American Conservative Union, which had been one of the plaintiffs in the *Buckley* v. *Vallejo* case (which established that candidates could spend unlimited amounts of their own funds on their campaigns and that organizations independent of a candidate's campaign could also spend limitless amounts). When the court decision came down in favor of our side, fully legitimizing independent campaign expenditures, we realized that we could run an independent campaign in support of Reagan, provided of course that we avoided all contact with his campaign, which we did. (I was not a great fan of the way John Sears was running the Reagan campaign, so it wasn't difficult for us to keep our distance.)

We felt strongly that if Reagan were to prevail over Ford, it wouldn't be sufficient to say simply, "He's better than Ford." Rather, we had to show that they had sharply different positions on such issues as the Panama Canal, Nelson Rockefeller's appointment as Vice President, Kissinger on foreign policy, SALT agreements, among other things. So, we made the theme of our independent campaign the headline in newspaper ads, THERE IS A DIFFERENCE. We also did radio spots in such states as North Carolina, Texas, and Indiana—all of which Reagan won. We were part of the mix, a small part.

The Federal Election Commission assumed that all of this was being done in cahoots with the Reagan campaign team. The FEC came in to the ACU to prove I was plotting with Sears! I tried to tell them they were barking up the wrong tree, but they looked for a conspiracy nevertheless—to no avail! I think that was the first independent campaign after the court ruling. Of course, it's quite common now.

My participation in that campaign was a manifestation of my regard for Reagan (Tom Winter, the editor of *Human Events*, organized the actual nuts and bolts of it).

Another thing I've always admired about him: He really believed in the so-called Eleventh Commandment ("Thou shall not speak ill of another Republican"). When he actually felt he had to criticize Ford, he looked physically uncomfortable. Even then, he was critical only of policy and issues. He never engaged in ad hominem criticism. That says a lot about his character and principles.

EDWIN J. FEULNER, JR.
PRESIDENT, THE HERITAGE FOUNDATION

"It wasn't an act he was putting on, it was him."

Ed Feulner has been president of the Heritage Foundation, one of Washington's largest "think tanks," since 1977. Before that he was executive director of the Republican Study Committee in the U.S. House of Representatives. In 1989, President Reagan awarded him the Presidential Citizens Medal. The citation notes: "By building an organization dedicated to ideas and their consequences, he has helped to shape the policy of our government. He has been a voice of reason and values in service to his country and the cause of freedom around the world." He is the author of several books and numerous monographs and newspaper and magazine articles. He holds a Ph.D. from the University of Edinburgh, Scotland.

It was early in the fall of 1978 when Richard Allen, then an informal foreign affairs adviser to Ronald Reagan, called me about a trip to Europe. He said former Governor Reagan would be in London for two days and asked if I could arrange something through my contacts with media people. I learned from Dick that only a breakfast meeting was available on Reagan's schedule. When I called around, I found that the reluctance of British journalists to indulge in what they considered to be a horrible American invention, the breakfast meeting, was overcome when they learned they would be meeting with the man who had tried in 1976 for the presidential nomination and just might have a political future.

I recall that Bill Deedes, the editor of the *Daily Telegraph* was there, as was Ferdie Mount, editor of *The Spectator*. There were also John O'Sullivan, Frank Johnson (then also of the *Telegraph*), and several others of my friends in the British press. Just before the Reagans came in, I recall, Ferdie Mount was saying, "Well, Feulner, I hope this is worth me having got up for."

After Governor Reagan had been introduced around, he plunged in with a few remarks, then went right to questions and answers. The refreshing candor with which he spoke—being, so to speak, from the real America and not the world of typical politicians—held the attention of these media people, and you could sense enthusiasm about him, in terms of his potential candidacy. They liked the way he talked about the special relationship among the United States and Britain and Europe and his references to past shared experiences. One of them said to me afterward that it was not only refreshing to hear a potential leader of the United States (and the free world) talk like this, but it was also reassuring to know that the "malaise" and confusion of Jimmy Carter's foreign policy could be replaced by something solid and dependable.

Another event I recall took place on October 22, 1983. About a month before, there was an interview of Mrs. Reagan having to do with future social engagements. She said that one of the most important events coming up was the tenth anniversary of the founding of the Heritage Foundation. We were of course delighted when the interview appeared in *The Washington Post*. And, at the banquet on that October evening, President Reagan talked about the foundation as being "the feisty new kid on the-conservative/Republican block" when it had been created a decade before, and the great help it had been to him over the years.

My wife, Linda, was seated next to him at the head table. When the color guard came in, he was beaming. She said he looked as if he enjoyed the pageantry, not of the presidency, but of what it symbolized about America. The guard presented the colors, then retreated. As they were leaving, President Reagan leaned over to Linda and whispered, "That was so moving, it makes me want to clap. Too bad no one else is." "Mr. President, I'll bet if you did it, everyone else would join in," she replied. He did and within a split second, fourteen hundred people were on their feet cheering.

That was a memorable evening for me, and when it was over, I said to Linda, "What was it like to sit next to the President? Did you talk about serious issues?" She said, "The only way I can describe it is that it was like talking with my father. President Reagan is 'real people.' He is interested in us and our children. He knew how many children we had. He knew they were both in high school and where they went to school. It was just like talking with a member of our family." I think the average American could sense this quality in Ronald Reagan; they could feel this man was real. He was like their father or their neighbor. He shared the same visions, the same concerns. It wasn't an act he was putting on. It was him.

GERALD R. FORD
THIRTY-EIGHTH PRESIDENT OF THE UNITED STATES

"The White House experience produces a special bond."

Gerald Ford earned his bachelor's degree from the University of Michigan, where he also was a star football player. He took his law degree at Yale.

Gerald Ford had just begun his law practice when World War II broke out. Discharged from the Navy as a lieutenant commander in 1946, he returned to the law practice, but in 1948, public service called and he was elected to the U.S. House of Representatives, where he served for the next twenty-five years. He became minority leader in 1965.

Upon the resignation of Spiro Agnew as Vice President in October 1973, "Jerry" Ford was nominated and confirmed to succeed him. A few months later, on August 9, 1974, he found himself the occupant of the Oval Office upon the resignation of President Richard Nixon. He presided for the next two and a half years—a very difficult time for the nation.

In fall 1974, he took the unpopular step of pardoning Richard Nixon. Nev-

ertheless, he went on to seek a full term as President in his own right. Ronald Reagan challenged him in a hard-fought race that did not end until the Republican National Convention in Kansas City in July 1976. President Ford emerged the nominee, losing one of the closest races in the nation's history to Jimmy Carter in November.

President Ford and his wife, Betty, have three sons and a daughter and five grandchildren.

The dedication of the Ronald Reagan Presidential Library in late 1991 in Southern California brought together then-President George Bush and four of us former Presidents, Ronald Reagan, Jimmy Carter, Richard Nixon, and myself. I remember that, at one point, Ron looked at all of us, grinned, and said, "I guess you and I have run against each other at least once." It was true, yet there we all were, the only people living to have shared the experience of serving in the White House as President.

Differences among people who have had this particular experience have a way of being put aside after the electoral battles are over. In the case of my contest with Jimmy Carter, it was pretty bitter. We strongly disagreed, especially on domestic policy. Yet, when the election was over (in a very tight race), we subsequently became good friends. I visited his library and museum in Atlanta and he came to Ann Arbor and Grand Rapids to my facilities. We've had a good relationship predicated, I think, on the fact we had both been President. Holding that office does create a tie between former Presidents, even though they might have had strong confrontations in the past.

The same thing happened between Ron Reagan and me. When he challenged me for the nomination in 1976, we had a head-to-head campaign that was finally settled by the delegates at the convention in Kansas City. Yet, after it was over, we developed a good and friendly relationship.

An incident comes to mind from the 1980 Republican convention in Detroit. Betty and I had planned to attend to show our support for the nominee, but did not expect to be active participants. We arrived on Sunday, the day before it began. So did the Reagans. Ron and Nancy called and asked if they might drop by to see us at our hotel. As they walked in, Ron handed me an Indian peace pipe. It was a gesture to lay the groundwork for his request at that meeting that I run as his vice presidential candidate. And, the peace pipe was also a symbol that we had put any past differences well behind us.

My joining the ticket did not work out subsequently, not because we disagreed on any issues, but because the role of the Vice President in our system is so fluid and uncertain. Just the same, I greatly appreciated his gesture. And, to this day, that peace pipe is prominently displayed in my office in California. I treasure it as a symbol both of our shared experiences and our friendship.

JAMES W. FULLER
BUSINESSMAN AND CAMPAIGN SUPPORTER

"His wife was still the most important thing in his life."

When the first incident Jim Fuller relates took place, he was a senior vice president of the New York Stock Exchange. He was later appointed by President Reagan to a term on the board of trustees of the Security Investors Protection Corporation. A native Californian, he is now a partner in a San Francisco investment firm.

It was October 1979 and Ronald Reagan was getting ready to announce his candidacy for the presidency. His exploratory committee had decided the announcement should be made in New York City. It was selected precisely because there was much reluctance in that part of the country to support his candidacy. Supporters of George Bush and John Connally said Reagan just wouldn't make it there, so the idea was to show that he could.

The event was to be a big dinner at the New York Hilton,

with Reagan's announcement speech as the highlight. Charles Wick pulled together a small planning committee whose job was to convince others to come to a meeting to hear Reagan and—we hoped—sign up to help make the event a success. Reagan had been warned in advance that this was a critical meeting and that many in attendance were skeptical of his chances.

He had been speaking for three or four minutes about his beliefs when a door opened in the back of the room and he stopped talking. "Excuse me, ladies and gentlemen, I must pause for a moment," he said. He left the podium and walked toward that door. None of us knew what was going on. Then, through the door came Nancy Reagan. He hugged and kissed her, escorted her to the front row, and said, "I apologize for the delay, but I didn't know she was coming and I missed her." We all clapped and I was deeply touched that this man felt so strongly about his wife and marriage that he would take time from a critically important meeting to greet her in such a special way. Winning the election was important to him, but his wife was still the most important thing in his life.

He ended up turning any skeptics in the room into supporters. The dinner was a success—nearly two thousand people attended.

Thinking back further, it was at a Nixon presidential campaign rally in 1968 in San Jose that I became convinced that Ronald Reagan would some day be President. He was governor of California then and was to introduce Nixon at this large rally. Sacramento was fogged in, however, so Reagan's plane couldn't take off.

The crowd was getting restless, so the organizers found someone else to introduce the candidate. Nixon gave a boring speech and the crowd seemed almost sleepy. But about halfway through, Governor Reagan arrived. They brought him up to the platform and sat him behind Nixon. He observed the crowd while Nixon finished to perfunctory applause. Mr. Nixon turned around and said, "Governor, I'm sorry you weren't here to give the introduction, but now that you are here, are there any comments you would like to make?" Reagan got up, approached the podium, and within three minutes, had the audience on its feet. People were laughing, cheering, applauding—mostly laughing at the spikes he was making about Nixon's opponent, Hubert Humphrey. I said to myself, "A man who can move an audience like that in such a short time is going to go a lot further than California." And, of course, history proved it so.

CHARLTON HESTON

FILM STAR

"I found Ronald Reagan to be a very skilled negotiator."

After starring in nearly sixty feature films and nearly as many theater productions, Charlton Heston says he can't remember ever wanting to be anything but an actor. He spent his early years in a small town in rural Michigan where his father ran a sawmill. He played in television dramas in the medium's early days, then began a Hollywood career marked by great versatility ("I've played cardinals and cowboys, kings and quarterbacks, presidents and painters, cops and con men, astronauts and geniuses," he says). He won the Academy Award for Best Actor in Ben-Hur in 1959. He served six terms as president of the Screen Actors Guild—a record. In the early 1960s he was active in the civil rights movement. Over the years he has undertaken a number of assignments involving the arts for various federal government agencies and departments.

Ronald Reagan and I first knew each other during our days in the Screen Actors Guild. By then he had more or less finished his film career and moved on to television. Still, he was carrying out his longtime commitment to the SAG. He appointed me to its board only a few months before he retired from its presidency. I've often said he was *my* President, long before he was the nation's.

Not long after he appointed me to the SAG board, we undertook the first strike in the Guild's history. It was very contentious. At stake was the question of actors' rights in the release of films to television. This was just beginning to happen. It was an entirely new situation. Ronald Reagan appointed me to the Guild's negotiating committee. There were three or four requisite unions for actors to join in those days, and I belonged to all of them. There was the SAG, of course, and the American Federation of Radio Artists (AFRA) and Actors' Equity. Also, I had been a founding member of a group attempting to organize actors in television. (By the way, when television began, the movie studios made the stupid mistake of pretending that the new medium didn't even exist!)

At the SAG, we were negotiating how to compensate actors in films that were just beginning to be released on television. The negotiating was fierce and it led to a strike—our first. During all this, I found Ronald Reagan to be a very skilled negotiator, not least because he was always good-humored. He would never take a confrontational position; he was not dogmatic. He might disagree, but he'd find a way to leave the other side with a feeling that they were good guys, too, and not the enemy. That is hard to do in such situations.

During any long union-management negotiations, especially with a strike going on, there are late night sessions; sometimes they last all night, because you're trying to resolve the situation. It's very tiring. By three in the morning, you've kicked your shoes off, taken off your coat and tie, and are sitting on couches drinking cold coffee, while the other side is out caucusing. Then, you pull yourself together when they come back into the room.

That hour of the morning can be an intimate time. It was the most intimate and personal time I had spent with Ronald Reagan. I think I learned something important about him then. I remember getting back home about four o'clock after one particular late-night session. I crept into the house, but my wife awoke and asked me how it went. "Oh, I don't know, honey," I replied. "We've got a lot of work to do. I don't see the end of this yet, but I'll tell you one thing: We have a President and we have a leader." Eight or ten years later, of course, the whole state, then later the whole country and the world knew it.

I recall, too, his 1984 reelection, his last run for public office. I was one of a number of surrogate speakers. A surrogate can be useful for getting a little extra media attention and, if well briefed, underscoring the candidate's message. But, a sitting President doesn't really need a lot of substantive help from friends who are well-known to the public. You're really backup.

At the end of that campaign, on the day before the election, he was going to have a rally in San Diego (where he had traditionally opened and closed his campaigns) and I was asked if I would like to come down and participate. Sure, I said.

During the campaign I had talked with Nancy several times and sensed she had some anxiety about the campaign. I had avoided talking with the President because I think one of the advantages of being able to talk to a President is that you don't do it, unless the house is burning down, so to speak.

In San Diego, there were thousands and thousands of people at the rally. They had parachutists, fireworks, the Marine Corps Band. There were a number of us surrogates and we each had our turn at the mike. Then, the President made what would be his last campaign speech. He blew everyone away! It was marvelous!

Nancy came up to me on the stage as everyone was milling around afterward and asked if I would like to go back to Los Angeles on *Air Force One*. That's an offer one doesn't turn down. Virtually everyone on the plane looked exhausted: Jim Baker, Ed Meese, Mike Deaver, even Nancy. The only one in high spirits was the President. He was older than anyone else aboard, but his eyes were shining and he made sure he talked with everyone on the plane.

Champagne was being poured and I asked Jim Baker what the outcome looked like for the next day. He said we'd probably lose Minnesota and the District of Columbia, but win everything else. I had thought it would be closer, but he said, "It's a lock, an absolute lock." And, as it turned out, he was right.

What I remember most is not that he had won by so much, but that to be successful in politics at that level you have to really love it—and Ronald Reagan did. It was the most fun he could imagine; to go out and campaign and say to people, "Let me tell you why I want you to vote for me and what my vision is for the country." Of course, he articulated that vision very, very well. He loved it. In fact, when we got off the plane that day in November 1984, he looked as if he could have started the whole thing over again.

My admiration for him is great. I think he's been one of our greatest Presidents. Forty or fifty years down the line, everyone will know it.

JACK KEMP
VICE PRESIDENTIAL NOMINEE, CABINET
SECRETARY, MEMBER OF CONGRESS

"The argument over his legacy is never ancient
history; it is always current."

*Republican nominee for Vice President of the United States of America in 1996,
Jack Kemp has been in public life for over three decades. A native Californian, he
was elected to Congress in 1970 from a Buffalo, New York, district after thirteen
years as a professional football quarterback. He played for the San Diego Chargers
from 1960 to 1962, then led the Buffalo Bills to a league championship in 1964.
(He was named Most Valuable Player in the league.) He then served nine terms
in the U.S. House of Representatives. In 1989, he became Secretary of Housing
and Urban Development in President George Bush's Cabinet. In 1993, he co-
founded Empower America, a public policy and advocacy organization dedicated to
expanding freedom, democratic capitalism, and economic growth.*

What are the most important aspects of Ronald Reagan's legacy? Ronald Reagan reduced political debates to their most fundamental level. Our view of the Reagan legacy predicts our entire view of political and economic challenges. If Reagan was right, liberals will always be wrong. So the argument over his legacy is never ancient history; it is always current.

Most politicians talk about policies and the changing issues of the day. Ronald Reagan talked about principles—deeply held beliefs. The difference is profound. Policies shift with the breeze of public opinion, but principles are anchors, even in a storm. Policies can be compromised, but principles are either obeyed or abandoned.

President Reagan remains controversial because he argued for a few simple—yet powerful—ideas on which it is still impossible to be neutral.

On economic matters, though he always hewed to the principle of increasing opportunities for people through economic growth, his views on how to accomplish this evolved. I saw a different Ronald Reagan after 1976. Previously, he had believed that balancing the federal budget was the way to stop inflation, after which taxes could be cut.

We had a recession in 1976, which was followed by the Carter years of a falling dollar, rising inflation, and unemployment and slow growth. It was called "stagflation."

During that 1976 recession, I studied the effects of the Kennedy tax cut of 1962–63 and became convinced that this was the way we should go to unleash the growth potential in the private sector without causing inflation. I proposed that income taxes be cut 30 percent in a single year. It was about then that I teamed up with Senator Bill Roth. We agreed that in order to get support on both sides of the aisle, we should stretch this out over three years at a rate of 10 percent each year. This became the keystone of the Kemp-Roth tax-cut plan.

I field-tested the concept in my district. Being a congressman from Buffalo, I had a large blue-collar constituency. I wanted to prove that reducing taxes across the board would be good not only for capital, but also for labor—working men and women. It was very popular. And, in those days, I won 70 percent of the votes in my district, so I knew we were on to something.

The International Longshoremen's Union endorsed me in 1978 and invited me to meet with their leader, Teddy Gleason, a rock-ribbed Irish-American patriot and staunch anti-Communist. His members were caught in "bracket creep," whereby their wage increases through contract negotiations threw them into ever-higher income-tax brackets (taxes weren't indexed in those days). I told him about my ideas for supply-side tax cuts. He liked them and invited me to speak to his members. My ILU speech was reprinted in *Human Events,* a publication Ronald Reagan read every week.

Next thing I knew, he called me. We talked about how supply-side tax cuts could benefit labor. Having headed a labor union himself and having majored in economics in college, he knew intuitively what we were talking about. He soon endorsed the Kemp-Roth plan and was the only national Republican leader to do so at the time.

Although his belief in economic stability and growth never changed, his view on how to get there did. He came to realize that cutting taxes—thereby unleashing human initiative and economic growth—would lead to a balanced budget. I asked him not to give me any credit for supply-side economics, for I had stolen it from JFK, who had stolen it from Ludwig Erhard, the architect of Germany's post–World War II recovery, who stole it from Calvin Coolidge, who finished the work of Warren Harding, who got it from Andrew Mellon, his treasury secretary. The idea was not new, but Ronald Reagan put his personal stamp on it, used his formidable communications and persuasion skills, and got it through Congress.

While we call it Reaganomics, it's really the classical prescription for economic growth: private ownership, free markets, sound money, lower taxes. And it has spread around the world. A few years ago, Senator Bill Armstrong and I took our wives to Russia to meet with Christians and Jews living in Moscow. While we were there, we met with the mayors of Moscow and St. Petersburg. They said to us, "Don't send us the economists from Harvard or Yale or the IMF, send us Ronald Reagan!" When you look around the world—from special enterprise zones along the south coast of China, to privatization going on nearly everywhere—you see the essence of Ronald Reagan's contribution to the economies of the world.

In the 1980 campaign, the same Teddy Gleason who had given me the opportunity to talk to his members endorsed Reagan. They had a lot in common: Irish roots, patriotism, both were FDR Democrats—and both realized we needed a new foreign policy. Gleason endorsed Reagan on the docks of Buffalo. From there, Reagan was to go to a labor luncheon, then fly to New Hampshire for his one-on-one debate with Bush.

During the Iowa campaign, just before the New Hampshire primary, Reagan had been advised not to be "too bold" because it could get him in trouble in the general election. He lost in Iowa. Well, I accompanied him to the airport. It was a twenty-minute ride. I wanted to make the most of it by emphasizing supply-side economics: sound, honest money and tax cuts across the board.

I'd just finished reading William Manchester's biography of General Douglas MacArthur, *American Caesar*. Manchester, a liberal, came to admire his subject. He also admired Winston Churchill. I said to Mr. Reagan, "Governor, do you remember Manchester's book on MacArthur?" He had read it. "Do you remember the part where he went to Tokyo to argue for the Inchon landing during the Korean War?" He said he did. I said, "In my view, the thirty percent cut in taxes is an Inchon landing for the Republican party, because it puts us on the offense and gets us off defense. That's exactly what MacArthur did." MacArthur had spent six hours in Tokyo, listening to Army, Navy, Air Force, State Department experts and all of Truman's advisers tell him why it wouldn't work. I said, "They told him the tides were wrong, the weather was wrong, he couldn't get his troops off the beach, and so forth.

"When MacArthur finally rose to his feet to speak, he felt the idea of the Inchon landing was slipping away. It was then that he recalled his father's words: 'Douglas, never forget, councils of war breed timidity and defeatism. You, Douglas, follow your instincts.' " He did and went forward with the landing. I reminded my audience of one that the Inchon landing was widely proclaimed to be one of the greatest military victories since Alexander the Great. I said to him, "It's your instincts that have gotten you to this point. You will be our nominee, but it's more important that you be our President. I hope the councils of war in this campaign get less attention than your instincts, because it's your instincts that will let you win."

In that debate, he instinctively went for the home run—the Inchon landing. And those instincts carried him through to success after success as President.

JEANE KIRKPATRICK
SCHOLAR, FORMER U.S. AMBASSADOR TO THE
UNITED NATIONS

"People who think he did not do his homework have not, themselves, done their homework."

The first woman to serve as the United States Representative to the United Nations, Jeane Kirkpatrick held that position for four years (1981–85)—with ambassadorial and Cabinet rank—in the Reagan administration. She was a member of the President's Foreign Intelligence Advisory Board (PFIAB) from 1985 to 1990 and Defense Policy Review Board (1985–93). She chaired the Commission on Fail-safe and Risk-reduction of the Nuclear Command and Control System in 1992. Following her service in the U.N., she resumed her position as Leavey Professor at Georgetown University and as senior fellow at the American Enterprise Insitute (AEI). She is the author of several books and a syndicated newspaper columnist. She holds a bachelor's degree from Barnard College and her master's and doctoral degrees from Columbia University.

It was not until 1980 that I met Ronald Reagan. Over the Christmas holiday in 1979, I received a letter from him about an article I had written in the December issue of *Commentary* magazine. When I saw the return address on the envelope, I thought it must have been misdirected, but I opened it. It was a rather long letter, single-spaced and clearly written by him. He wrote that he had read my article with great interest. He then addressed several aspects of the problems in Central America. He did so in sincere language and a straightforward manner. He asked if I would be willing to meet him at some point to discuss these issues.

I was frankly surprised that Ronald Reagan had read this rather complicated, long article, "Dictatorships and Double Standards." I learned later from Dick Allen that he had given him a copy of it as Reagan was leaving Washington. Apparently, he had to change planes in Chicago, because he called Dick from there and said, "Who is he?" "Who is who?" Dick said. "Who is this Jeane Kirkpatrick?" To which Dick said, "Well, *he* is a she." So, obviously, he had a lively interest in this article, as he expressed in his letter to me.

Till then, I had never been particularly interested in Ronald Reagan. I had been a lifelong Democrat and knew very few Republicans.

Two or three weeks after receiving the letter, I wrote him a note and said I would be happy to meet with him in Washington. Not long after that, Dick called to say there was going to be a small group meeting with Mr. Reagan at the Madison Hotel to discuss foreign policy. I spent a couple of hours with him and the group that afternoon, and that evening I was at dinner with him at George Will's home. From this I gained a clear impression of him and liked him. He was very different from the other major political figures I had known. Till then, the most important ones in my life had been Hubert Humphrey and "Scoop" Jackson. One of the things I liked about Ronald Reagan was his directness. He didn't speak to you as if he were speaking to a crowd. He spoke to you in a very direct, personal fashion. I sensed from the beginning that he was sensitive to other people. All my later dealings with him confirmed that.

Most of my early conversations with him after that were concerned with Central and South America. Something else he brought up, though, was that he, too, had been a Democrat. He talked about his experiences with the Screen Actors Guild and their struggle with Communists infiltrating the Hollywood unions. He said that he ultimately changed parties not because he had changed his mind, but because the party had shifted. I felt very much the same. He understood well the phenomenon of the Reagan Democrat, because he was the first one! Some friends of mine said he was also the first neoconservative. In any case, he was at pains to emphasize to me that there would be no embarrassment in changing parties.

When he called me to ask me to be his U.S. ambassador to the United Nations, it came out of the blue. No one had called me in advance to sound me out. I had read in *The Washington Post* that someone else (who wanted the job very much) was under discussion, but that Reagan had another person in mind. My name wasn't mentioned in the story. Then he called me and with his usual graciousness and warmth asked if I would do this. I said I wasn't sure. This wasn't the type of job for which I had any real preparation, except that I was studying the countries of the world. I had no diplomatic background. I was an academic, an intellectual.

He responded by saying he felt sure I would be able and well prepared, and, he added, he very much wanted me to do it. So I said, "Mr. President, if you really do feel confident that this is a job I can do as you would like me to, then I accept." He said, "Jeane, you've made my day."

By then, I had met him a dozen or more times since that first meeting in early 1980, because I had become active in his campaign. When I joined his foreign policy task force, it was the first real contact I had ever had with a Republican campaign in my life. The first time I went to a meeting of this group and was surrounded by all those Republicans, I did feel embarrassed. He knew that, and put me at ease with some gentle teasing.

Once he was in office, I saw him fairly frequently in the context of the Cabinet and the National Security Council. He was very well informed and always well prepared. People who think he did not do his homework have not, themselves, done their homework.

He had made it clear to me that I could see him any time. I never wanted to abuse that privilege and I never did. I would see him alone perhaps once or twice during a U.N. term. We would discuss his priorities in the General Assembly and what I thought the principal forthcoming issues would be. I would review various opportunities with him to make sure I was on the right track. I always got 100 percent support from President Reagan. I never was given detailed instructions by him. I had a clear understanding about the direction and goals and priorities that we would pursue in the next month or two, or whatever the time frame was. I found him supportive, reinforcing, and wonderful to work with. We had complete understanding about where we were going. I understood that my job was to try to achieve our goals and do it as effectively as I could.

What turned out to be a very controversial U.N. resolution early in his first term involved Israel's bombing of the Iraqi nuclear reactor. Ronald Reagan detested the use of force. He admired Israel, but he disapproved of its preemptive use of force. He said he understood their concerns, but he didn't want to begin his term leaving the impression that he was always (and automatically) going to take Israel's side and never look at the Arab side. On the other hand, he didn't like condemning Israel and he didn't want the Israelis to suffer any truly negative consequences, because he understood the danger they were in from Iraq. Nevertheless, he didn't want the United States to be in the position of having to veto a resolution, if that could be avoided.

He asked me to attempt to negotiate a resolution that we condemn the bombing without damaging Israel. That was no mean trick, as it turned out. I spent two or three days in a room with the Iraqi foreign minister. He wasn't easy to deal with. Finally, a legal adviser from the U.S. Mission to the U.N. helped me work out an agreement on a resolution that was critical without being threatening. The President was pleased with the outcome; his objective had been achieved. At the next Cabinet meeting, he put his arm around me and called me his "heroine"—which of course delighted me. I found him to be very generous with praise.

At Christmas one year, he gave all of us one of those signs, etched in glass, that read, "It doesn't matter who gets the credit, so long as the job gets done."

His style of management was to identify a job to be done, find the person to do it, then let them do it. This is the best approach for a President, I believe, because no President can possibly do a significant part of the many jobs himself. He can't track all the strategies, events, and problems that require attention and make all the decisions by himself. I think the most important single quality in any President is the ability to choose competent people, then let go and let them do the job. I think Ronald Reagan is the kind of manager the presidency needs. He and Franklin Roosevelt and Dwight Eisenhower shared these characteristics. I think he has yet to get the credit he deserves for his success as a manager.

I had been thinking about this subject back in early 1980 when I was trying to decide whether to take the step of supporting my first Republican for President. I decided to call my good friend Jesse Unruh, then California's state treasurer and former speaker of the assembly. (In 1970, when Reagan was seeking reelection as governor, Jesse had run against him.) My question to Jesse was, "Can he govern the country?"

Jesse Unruh, Reagan's old rival, had this to say: "He wasn't the best governor California ever had but he wasn't the worst by a long shot." He went on to tell me that early in his first term, Reagan had little understanding of the job of governing and working with a legislature (and this one was controlled by the Democrats). "Before long," Jesse said, "he understood we had to work together on problems. Once he understood that, he did a workmanlike job." Jesse and I agreed that Ronald Reagan had done a more effective job of getting along with a Democratic legislature in California than Democrat Jimmy Carter had done with a Democratic legislature in Georgia and a Democratic Congress in Washington. Coming from such a partisan as Jesse, that was real praise. In short, Ronald Reagan could compromise but remain true to his principles.

HELMUT KOHL
CHANCELLOR OF THE FEDERAL REPUBLIC
OF GERMANY

"Ronald Reagan meant what he said, and he was right."

Chancellor since 1982, Helmut Kohl has been in office the longest of any leader among the Western industrialized nations. Before taking office, he led the parliamentary opposition party, the CDU/CSU (Christian Democratic Union/Christian Social Union) from 1976. The stationing of cruise missiles in Germany, as a counterweight to Soviet missiles (in the face of strong opposition) took place early in his tenure. And the reunification of East and West Germany has taken place under his leadership.

Active in politics and government all his adult life, Chancellor Kohl studied law and government at the Universities of Frankfurt and Heidelberg.

One of my most vivid memories of Ronald Reagan is of his visit to the Brandenburg Gate in Berlin in 1987.

At that time, the people of Berlin were celebrating the 750th birthday of their city, which was still divided by the Wall and barbed wire. The cold war was not yet over, the medium-range nuclear missiles were still in position, and the Soviet Union had not yet agreed to real disarmament.

On June 12 1987, President Reagan addressed all Berliners, Germans, and Europeans. He spoke of unity and freedom, standing on the border which the Communists had turned into a military fortification that still divided Berlin, Germany, and Europe. On the other side of the Wall, in East Berlin, armed border guards watched the proceedings from their towers. Their binoculars were turned toward us, underscoring their distance—but also their curiosity.

In West Berlin, however, the usual, almost routine protests against the American guest were in progress. The President of the country that, like no other, had protected Berlin and guaranteed its freedom for forty years, gave this reply in front of the Brandenburg Gate: "If those demonstrators had the kind of government they apparently seek, none of them would be able to do what they are doing." How many people in the West, in Germany, too, had let themselves be intimidated by the Wall and the rulers behind it? How many had lost heart? But Ronald Reagan did not accept such resignation. He had come to Berlin neither to accuse nor to lament, but to convey a message of hope. "There is only one Berlin. Freedom is the victor," he said. And, one thing was certain: If the Soviet Union did not make fundamental changes, it would become obsolete.

The entire world recalls the appeal Ronald Reagan made that day: "Mr. Gorbachev, open this gate! Mr. Gorbachev, tear down this wall!" Many have long since forgotten or dismissed from their minds the fact that at that time they were amused or even felt embarrassed by these words. They were unable to differentiate between the spirit of the cold war and a sense of values, between wisdom and a lack of realism. Their reactions at the time were a manifestation of that all-too-common confusion and self-delusion that have made it so hard for free nations to hold their own in difficult times.

Ronald Reagan meant what he said, and he was right. His

speech is permanent testimony to his belief in the power of freedom: "This wall will fall, for it cannot withstand faith. It cannot withstand truth. The wall cannot withstand freedom." This was no rash prophecy but the firm conviction of an American President who saw in Berlin the qualities that had made his own country great: creativity, willpower, courage, and the love of freedom.

Today we know that the final phase of the East-West conflict began in 1987. How important it was, at that particularly critical time, to profess the credo for the free world! In welcoming President Reagan to Berlin, I said, "Peace can only flourish where the rule of law and human rights prevail."

Ronald Reagan demonstrated the sovereignty of democracy and the self-confidence of the leader of the free world. There is no middle course between freedom and dictatorship, and we shall never cease to declare our commitment to our common values. That was our joint message that day, and it was—and will continue to be—the cornerstone of German-American friendship.

DAVID LAUX
FORMER DIRECTOR OF ASIAN AFFAIRS,
NATIONAL SECURITY COUNCIL

"He said, 'We're going to give her asylum if I have
to adopt her and make her part of my own family.' "

From mid-1982 through 1986, David Laux was the director of Asian Affairs at the National Security Council in the White House. His portfolio included Chinese affairs (the China Mainland—PRC, Taiwan, Hong Kong, Mongolia, Macao), as well as Australia, New Zealand, Pacific island nations and the Trust Territory of Pacific Islands (Micronesia). He was responsible for planning the President's personal involvement in U.S. relations with these countries. After leaving the NSC, through mid-1990 he was chairman and managing director of the American Institute in Taiwan, which is under contract to the U.S. Department of State to manage the unofficial commercial, trade, and cultural relations between the people of the United States and those of Taiwan. Since late 1990, he has been president of the USA-ROC Economic Council, an American organization concerned with U.S.-Taiwan trade and business matters.

Thinking back, nothing annoyed me more than the occasional innuendoes in the press that Ronald Reagan was "packaged" for the presidency by the Republican party and Hollywood promoters and didn't have a brain in his head. In reality, although he wasn't an intellectual, he symbolized the values of America. He had an instinctive sense of what was right, and he used it.

In my experience of four and a half years on the National Security Council staff, he always did his homework. Before a meeting he read the briefing materials, thought about them, and often did his own research, contacting people on the outside for input. He was not a prisoner of his staff. He'd listen to everybody, reflect, and then, if he thought more information was needed, would say something along the lines of "We don't know enough about 'x' or 'y.' Let's get Defense to learn more about 'x' and State to do a little more research on 'y.' Then, let's meet again in two weeks and have another look at it." Toward the end of the meeting, if he saw that someone hadn't spoken, he'd call on them to make sure he had everyone's views. Sometimes he would say, "I want to sleep on this before making a decision." While he was great at delegating, he knew when to step in and take hold: to make a decision or emphasize a point. He had a sense of balance there. In matters of foreign policy, Ronald Reagan had a sure sense of America's strategic priorities, a sense of proportion, and an instinct for the right thing to do.

In Asia, for example, he understood that our top priority was our relationship with Japan, not China. Americans have historically gotten romantically and emotionally more involved with China. Just about everyone is interested in China—much more so than Japan. The amount of literature about China far exceeds what we have on Japan. And, someday, if China ever gets its act together and becomes a truly homogeneous nation—highly organized, with advanced technology—it could be the world's leading power. Meanwhile, during President Reagan's administration, Japan's economic power, financial strength, and technological know-how made it of much more immediate importance. If any single feature characterized Reagan's Asian foreign policy, this was it.

He recognized that our security interests with respect to Japan more than balanced our trade deficit concerns and all the complaints of the Japan-bashers. There was a constant fight over this, but the President understood deeply the benefits we had in this close relationship with Japan.

He also understood the significance of Japan's accomplishment in surpassing the Soviet Union as an economy. Even though Japan was only one two-hundredth the size geographically, had only 40 percent as much population, and virtually no natural resources—whereas the USSR was loaded with resources—when it became clear they were going to surpass the Soviet Union in terms of economic production, it proved the free world's point: that freedom, democracy, and a market economy were better guaranties for human prosperity than was communism. We never made enough of this in a public relations sense, but Ronald Reagan understood it very well. He also knew that the United States and Japan together had the economic clout to carry the rest of the world. He had a very special relationship with Prime Minister Nakasone, and that was an asset, too.

Reagan also understood the importance of China, even though in an election campaign speech in August 1980 he raised what Chinese authorities thought was the specter of reestablishing official relations with the Republic of China on Taiwan. As soon as he took office, however, he quietly reassured China that he understood the fundamental importance of good relations between that country and the United States and he took steps to advance them. During his first year in office, he sent reassuring messages by way of former President Ford, Vice President Bush, and Secretary of State Haig.

During the 1980 campaign, the Chinese embassy in Washington was reporting to the leadership in Beijing that they need not worry about Reagan's campaign rhetoric because Carter was going to be reelected. Beijing was shocked when that didn't occur. They had to refocus. They watched the first moves of the new administration carefully and made their own deliberations on how to deal with us. They decided to play hardball. At the economic conference in Cancun, Mexico, in October 1981, they made that clear. In effect, they said, "Until we get an agreement about arms sales to Taiwan, we are going to put everything important in our relations on the shelf. We will not send any visitors to the United States of the rank of vice minister or higher, and we will not receive any of your officials of the rank of assistant secretary or above, and we are halting negotiations on nuclear and other matters until we reach agreement on the Taiwan arms sales issue." What followed was ten months of tough negotiations that resulted in the Taiwan Arms Sales Communiqué of August 17, 1982. It represented a compromise by both sides. President Reagan felt strongly that the problems between the China mainland and Taiwan were a "family" matter and that the United States should not get involved, beyond expressing our overriding concern that any settlement be peaceful. He also felt that, while our relationship with China was important, we should not cultivate it by weakening our relationship with Taiwan. That was consistent with his long-held views. In his words, "We won't make new friends at the expense of old ones."

He believed it was essential that we keep this complicated and difficult two-track relationship in balance. He stuck to that principle of balance throughout his presidency, and we had a better policy in those years than we have had since. The Taiwan Arms Sales Communiqué made the point that we would limit the size of our arms sales and technology to Taiwan to what we had done in earlier years. We would gradually reduce sales over time, although the communiqué did not spell out details. In return, China would take a more peaceful approach to Taiwan.

President Reagan briefed congressional leaders after approving this communiqué. He said that the quality of arms and level of technology we would continue to provide Taiwan would give them the capability to fend off any attempt at a military invasion, but if the equation of military balance changed in the future—either because China began to develop advanced weapons or bought them from elsewhere (such as the Soviet Union)—he was prepared to take another look and make any adjustments that were necessary to make sure there continued to be a rough balance of power in the Taiwan Strait. That's very important, but not very well known. Later, during the Bush administration, China purchased SU-27s from the Soviets, was sniffing around exploring the possibility of buying a surplus aircraft carrier, was developing an in-air refueling capability, and made threatening noises about the Spratly Islands in the South China Sea. All of these things contributed to President Bush's approving the sale of F-16s to Taiwan late in his own administration.

Leading up to a visit by China's Premier Zhao Ziyang in January 1984, we had two National Security Council meetings to make sure that all Cabinet officers and departments involved in the visit would be singing from the same sheet of music, so to speak. Toward the end of one of those sessions, President Reagan said, "I don't know if the rest of you remember this, but after the Boxer Rebellion in 1900, all the European states imposed indemnities on Beijing to pay for damages, and so forth. They collected these and used them. We also had one set up, but used the proceeds for scholarships to send Chinese students to the United States. A lot of good things came out of that gesture, and I think it showed we were different from the European powers in not having any predatory designs on China. I hope the Communist leaders who are coming to visit us will remember that." I was floored. I had prepared his briefing papers for this meeting and this wasn't in them. He had recalled this from his own research. An associate, recounting a similar experience when Reagan was on his way to Taiwan for a visit in the late 1970s, recalled him noting that the United States had never been a colonial power in China, that the Chinese word for America was mei-gwo (meaning "beautiful country"), and that our people went to China primarily as doctors, teachers, and missionaries, to help the people.

I recall another case in our relations with China that illustrated President Reagan's sense of principles. In late 1982, Hu Na, a nineteen-year-old tennis player, had just defected from China and asked for asylum in the United States. There was a big debate

among the concerned parties inside our government whether to
grant it. Some felt that, as a teenage athlete, she didn't have a
political thought in her head and didn't, therefore, qualify for
"political asylum."

They also believed she would not be persecuted if she were
sent back home. Others felt it was very important that we grant
her asylum—for the symbolism of our role as a sanctuary and
land of freedom. Judge William Clark, then the national security
adviser, gave me the task of doing a survey of the views of the
relevant government bureaus and agencies involved. At the State
Department, I found that four bureaus were split evenly, two for
asylum and two against, but that they had not yet reached a de-
partmental conclusion. Judge Clark sent my survey in to the President. Shortly after, Reagan gave his decision. He said, "We're
going to give her asylum if I have to adopt her and make her a
part of my own family." She was granted asylum.

Ronald Reagan paid attention to other parts of the Pacific,
too. Australia was an example. He had a strong memory of the
United States and Australia fighting side by side in World War
II and he wanted to promote our relationship with this ally. He
and Australian Prime Minister Bob Hawke really hit it off, and
developed a strong personal relationship. On the occasion of one
1985 visit by Hawke to Washington, I recall participating in an
early meeting with Hawke and our secretary of agriculture.
Hawke fought for every word he could get on wheat and cattle
into the joint communiqué that was to be issued later in the visit.
I was surprised that Hawke was dealing with it rather than leaving
it to his own minister of agriculture, who had accompanied him.
So in my briefing paper for President Reagan for his own meeting
with Hawke, I made a point of this and emphasized it to John
Poindexter, who was then the national security adviser and
would be conducting our briefing of the President. John didn't
always like to bother the President with what he thought were
details. By the time the meeting was drawing to a close, he hadn't
raised it. I slipped John a note. He looked at me and I made a
face, attempting to emphasize the importance of this concern of
Hawke's. The President noticed my body language and said,

"David, you have something on your mind. What is it?" So I told him, and he appreciated it. I mention this only to emphasize that, as a staff member, I was always impressed with the President's sensitivity to everyone who was in a meeting with him. If he saw anyone there who seemed anxious to say something, he figured it must be important, so drew it out.

Big countries were not his only concern. He also cared about the problems of small countries and our relations with them. In the South Pacific, most of the island groups that had been colonies had become independent in the 1970s and early 1980s. I researched the history of our relations with these small island countries and found we had never invited a South Pacific island national leader to the United States for an official visit. I wrote a memo on this, suggesting we could strengthen our relationships with the island nations by inviting a leader for an "official working visit." President Reagan approved the proposal and we selected Ratu Mara, the prime minister of Fiji, who was regarded as the senior statesman in the region. Reagan handled the November 1984 visit beautifully. This visit said to every small country in the Pacific that we cared about them and that we had time to learn about their interests and concerns.

Mongolia was another case. Recognition had been under consideration for a number of years, but had never been brought to fruition, for a variety of reasons. The State Department had trained a couple of foreign service officers in the language, to be geared up to start an embassy, should the recognition ever occur. We reviewed the situation and I wrote a memo recommending diplomatic recognition. It came back with a note from the President that read, "You're absolutely right. Get together with State on this and let's get cracking." We did, and the recognition took place—another accomplishment of his administration. The Pacific islands and Mongolia were certainly not the biggest things on the foreign policy platter, but his actions told me that here was a man who paid close attention to the smaller responsibilities, just as he did the biggest ones.

He also knew how to use his acting experience to communicate his sincere interest in people. An example comes to mind that involved Peter Coleman, then the governor of American Samoa, who in 1982 was to host an annual Pacific Forum conference of all the islands in the South Pacific. He had written to request a letter from the President to be read at the meeting. I was new at the NSC then, learning about the resources available at the White House, when I discovered the President did videotaped messages for special occasions. Every two or three weeks, he would tape somewhere between three and ten at one sitting. So I requested one in place of a letter for this conference and drafted the script. When I saw the result on the video monitor, I could hardly believe my eyes and ears. The President put such feeling and sincerity into his message that you would have thought that, from his earliest years, the Pacific Forum was the subject he was most interested in! This was one of many examples where his film, television, and radio background made his communications so effective. Peter Coleman was ecstatic. He told me afterward that the videotape was the highlight of the plenary session of the Forum.

Later, I talked with the video producers and asked them how the President did it. "He's a genius," one of them said. "Most politicians we've worked with have to do it nine or ten times before it comes out right. President Reagan reads the script once, makes mental notes as to when to make pauses, where to place emphasis, and when to look the camera right in the eye to make a point. He almost always gets it 'right on' the first time."

In his sense of values and morality—of what was right for the nation—he represented the heart of America. He gave us a renewed sense of hope and self-respect. And he garnered great respect for America from abroad. I think he was a great President and believe he'll go down in history that way.

PAUL LAXALT
UNITED STATES SENATOR (1974–86)

"He was a great President because he is a great man."

Ronald Reagan and his closest political friend, Paul Laxalt, became governors of their respective states, California and Nevada, in 1967. Among other issues, they worked together for the creation of the bistate Tahoe Regional Planning Agency, to oversee the development of the Lake Tahoe Basin in the Sierra Nevada. Paul Laxalt, as a U.S. senator, chaired three Reagan presidential campaigns, in 1976, 1980, and 1984, and was general chairman of the national Republican party from 1983 to 1987. In 1986, he was President Reagan's personal emissary to President Ferdinand Marcos of the Philippines, eventually urging the Philippine leader to step down peacefully to avoid a civil war. Since retiring from the Senate, he has headed the Laxalt Group in Washington, D.C.

Ronald Reagan and I probably first met at one of those political candidate "cattle shows" in the mid-1960s in Nevada or California. I recall vividly working with him during the Goldwater presidential campaign in 1964. That was the year he gave that memorable television address that brought him to national attention politically. Never have I seen such an outpouring of support resulting from a single political speech.

In 1966, we were both elected governors. We forged a close personal friendship as we worked together on matters affecting both states. I discovered early on that Ronald Reagan was not terribly comfortable with other politicians. This was particularly apparent to me at the governors conferences we attended. As a result, I volunteered to serve as his unofficial "bridge" to the other governors.

In 1974, I was elected to the U.S. Senate. At this time, he and I stayed in touch, but our friendship became much closer when he asked me to chair his campaign for the presidency in 1976. It had become increasingly clear that he was serious about challenging Gerald Ford for the Republican nomination. The thought of taking on a sitting Republican President was somewhat intimidating, but I thought that Ronald Reagan had the right prescription for our ailing nation at that difficult time in its history.

It was an incident during that campaign that confirmed to me that I had made the right decision by supporting him. At the Republican National Convention in Kansas City, our situation had become desperate. Our delegate counters told us that President Ford was on the verge of securing the nomination. Reagan had named his running mate, Senator Richard Schweiker of Pennsylvania, in advance, as a means of keeping momentum and possibly gaining more delegates. But now in Kansas City, Dick Schweiker had concluded that he was hurting Reagan's chances of winning the nomination. The Schweiker selection had itself been a politically dangerous move because he was—unfairly, in my view—considered anathema to many conservatives.

The senator said to Governor Reagan, "I think I've become a liability to this ticket and respectfully request to be replaced." Ronald Reagan, facing a desperate situation, could have taken the easy route and granted the senator's request. Instead, without hesitating, he said, "No, Dick. We came to Kansas City together and we're going to leave together."

Reagan's decision, as it turned out, sealed any hopes he had of winning the nomination. But, from that moment, my respect and admiration for Ronald Reagan never wavered—this was not politics as usual!

The same basic decency that Ronald Reagan exhibited on that day in Kansas City was, I believe, an important reason why he became such a beloved President. The American people understood that their Commander in Chief, although not infallible, was a kind, decent, and courageous man who shunned political expediency in order to do what he believed was right.

He was a great President because he is a great man.

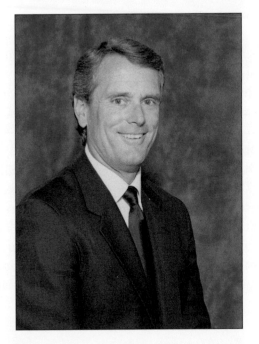

DENNIS LE BLANC
FORMER AIDE

"We've got to do something about this."

On graduating from Sacramento State University in 1971, Dennis LeBlanc joined the California State Police and was assigned to Governor Reagan's security detail through his second term. In 1975, he joined Deaver and Hannaford, to "advance" the travel and events of the firm's major client, Ronald Reagan. In 1981–82, he was a special assistant to the President in the Military Office at the White House. Since 1983, he has been an executive of the Pacific Telesis Group, first in Washington, now in Sacramento.

Two things stand out. In 1975, right after he'd finished his second term as governor and we were working out of the Deaver & Hannaford office in Los Angeles, Governor Reagan and I were on the road for his first trip on the speaking circuit. At the time, I wasn't married, but my future wife, Sue, and I were dating. Customarily, I would telephone her every night to see how she was doing.

We had been on the road three or four days when we got to Chicago, where we were to spend the night at the Hyatt Regency Hotel. I don't recall the group Governor Reagan was to speak to the next day, but I do remember calling Sue that night. Her reply was "Don't talk to me." I thought, "What did I do?" She slammed the phone down, so I called her back. She told me I had forgotten to call her on Valentine's Day. That didn't seem like a big deal to me, but it obviously was to her.

The next morning, out of the blue, Mr. Reagan asked me, "How's Sue doing?" I said, "Believe it or not, Governor, she's not speaking to me." Since this was man-to-man, I figured he would see my point of view when I told him the cause: that I had forgotten Valentine's Day. "You didn't!" he said. "We've got to do something about this." So, he took me down to the flower shop in the lobby. He ordered a dozen red roses and, on the card, he wrote, "Dear Sue, Dennis and I are sorry. Will you please be his Valentine?—Ronald Reagan." He sent them to her at the state senator's office in Sacramento where she worked. That night I called her and I got both forgiveness and excitement. He had bailed me out—and it was terrific for a young man in love.

In August 1977, after I left Deaver & Hannaford and my advance and security work for Mr. Reagan, our twin boys were born. I thought back to that Valentine's Day and that, before I went to the hospital to see Sue and the boys, I had better stop by and get flowers. Even though I hadn't had contact with Governor Reagan for four or five months, when I walked into Sue's room, there were flowers from him. His note read, "Dennis, you know I'm sorry that I kept you away from Sue for so long. You'll have to start providing backups for your original child." (He knew my security procedures by then.) It was a wonderful touch. Those twin boys started college in the fall of 1995.

ART LINKLETTER
RADIO AND TELEVISION STAR, AUTHOR,
PHILANTHROPIST, BUSINESS EXECUTIVE

"It struck me how little changed he was, upon
becoming President."

*Art Linkletter was born in Moose Jaw, Saskatchewan, Canada, where, as an
orphan, he was adopted by a Baptist minister, the Reverend Fulton Linkletter,
and his wife. They moved to California when Art was a schoolboy. He graduated
from high school and college in San Diego, intending to become a college professor.
Instead, he was offered a radio announcer's job, took it, and was launched on a
sixty-plus-year career in radio and television. Two of his best-known shows were
the long-running* Art Linkletter's House Party *on CBS and* People Are Funny
*on NBC. He is the author of twenty-four books, the recipient of ten honorary
degrees, active in numerous philanthropic activities, and, as chairman of Linkletter
Enterprises, a successful businessman.*

I knew the young Ronald Reagan when he was making pictures and was just beginning to get his toes onto the top rungs of the business. We lived in the same neighborhood. When I first knew him, he was married to Jane Wyman. We were both family guys; we didn't drink or go out with wild men, so a good evening on the town would be for them and their kids and Lois and me and our kids to go down to Will Wright's ice cream store.

I got to know him quite well as he rose in the film business. We both belonged to professional groups such as the Friars and we often found ourselves seated next to each other on daises at "roasts." He was a great storyteller, and that's my business, too. We were both good at it, but different from most of the others because we didn't do dirty stuff. Those stag roasts got pretty raunchy, since many of the stars who were good at it had come up through vaudeville, which we hadn't. They were used to raw material. So Ron and I found ourselves in the same boat. I never heard him tell a story you couldn't repeat almost anywhere.

Then I got to know Nancy, by chance, before they were married. Sometimes, in my lectures around the country, people will ask me about famous people—"Do you know the Reagans?" for example—and I'll reply, "Nancy Reagan was my wife at one time." The audience will gasp in surprise until I tell them it was for only thirty minutes when we were starred together in a *General Electric Theater* show on CBS. We played in a drama titled "The Odd Ball," in which she had a son who was a rascal, and I had a daughter I was trying to protect from him. We were enemies at first, but finally ended up being a romantic example. She was Nancy Davis, of course, then.

I had an interesting experience involving Disney in the early 1950s. Walt Disney asked me to be master of ceremonies at the opening of Disneyland. He said, "Pick a couple of your friends and we'll all go down there to Anaheim and have some fun." So I asked Bob Cummings and Ron. The four of us (including Walt) made history by opening that first Disney theme park. They still show some film clips of that event with me saying, "Ron, run over and see if you can find so-and-so." Remember, I was the emcee. That always gets people since, after all, he's been President. Imagine me giving him orders!

Then he went on television for General Electric and gave speeches at GE plants around the country. That was the first indication that he had more to say than just as a character in a movie. People began to talk about him as a possible candidate for office. The Republicans were always looking for supporters from Hollywood. There weren't many of us: John Wayne, Jimmy Stewart, Henry Fonda, and me. Not many others. Most every one else was a liberal Democrat. Ron Reagan had changed from Democrat to Republican by the early 1960s because his ideology was conservative.

When the circle of friends who later became his "kitchen cabinet" urged him to run for governor, I recall, Nancy was taken aback when I suggested he should do something else. My argument was that it was like being the chairman of a very large corporation, full of administrative details. "People like Ron and me are communicators above all, not administrative types." Nancy said, "Well, he's been president of the Screen Actors Guild." I said that couldn't be compared with being governor of a state that was comparable with a country that had the sixth or seventh largest economy in the world. "Well, what do you think he should do?" she asked. I said he should run for U.S. Senate. "He should be there with ideas and persuasiveness. I've known some governors and they all told me what a miserable job it was." Well, I later ate my words. I emceed the opening event of his campaign for governor in Los Angeles.

He was a good governor. He accomplished a lot. He took advice from people who had business experience, and the state of California is a very big business. Then, of course, came the time when he was going to run for President. I remember appearing with him at the Hollywood Bowl and elsewhere. I was delighted when he was elected.

He appointed me to a presidential commission on recreation and health. I had been in the White House before that many times, was a friend of Richard Nixon's, and had known Truman and Eisenhower. (I owned a publishing company and worked with Truman on a book at one time.) It struck me how little changed Reagan was, upon becoming President. He and Truman changed the least. When I would go to the White House, Reagan would say, "Art, I've got a new story for you." I recall one time we were standing in one of the main rooms there. We had just finished a meeting of the recreation commission, of whom George Allen, the famous coach of the Washington Redskins, was then chairman. Reagan and I got to talking. Photographers were snapping pictures from about fifteen feet away. When we were alone, I called him Ron, Ronnie, or Dutch, but when people were around, I called him "Mr. President." So, I said, "Dutch, what do you do nights here? You can't just go out to a movie like we used to, and there aren't always state dinners." He said, "Art, I work out. I have a set of these modern workout machines. After I've been cooped up all day, I work out like a demon." He told me he thought he was in better shape than he had ever been and invited me to feel his chest muscles! I laughed and said, "Are you kidding? If I did that, either the Secret Service would be all over me or people would think we were getting intimate!" "All right, then," he said, "feel my arm." Sure enough, it was solid as a rock.

When I'd talk to him on the phone occasionally from Hollywood, he'd always start the conversation the same way: "First, before we get to business, do you have a story for me?" He was always collecting stories.

Late in his second term, he asked me to be our commissioner general to the World's Fair in Brisbane, Australia, with the rank of ambassador. The fair was to celebrate Australia's 150th anniversary. I told him that Dick Nixon had asked me to be ambassador to Australia because I had a number of sheep stations and was well known there. I begged off because I was so busy with the work of the President's Commission on Drug Abuse, of which I was a member. I was speaking out on the subject at high schools and colleges, because I had lost my daughter to drugs and I had a deep commitment to reaching young people. (I also wrote a book, *Drugs at My Door Step*.) I asked President Nixon if he'd rather have me sitting in some distant embassy, or spending my time trying to save kids from this rising tide of drug abuse. He understood, and I stayed home.

Now, years later, I found myself in this special ambassadorial role. I had to be confirmed by the Senate Foreign Relations Committee. The State Department sent over half a dozen young men to prepare me for the hearing. When we got there, one of the senators said, "Art Linkletter, I always used to watch your shows when I was a kid and, as far as I'm concerned, you can be anything you like." That was it. We were out in about five minutes.

Since then, Ronald Reagan and I have seen each other from time to time since he left the White House. I was honorary president of the International Swimming Hall of Fame. Former Treasury Secretary Bill Simon and I had both received its International Swimming Award, which is given to swimmers who were good competitors and who went on to success or fame in some other field, and we decided to give it to Reagan. I appeared at his office in Los Angeles. A group of swimming and diving champions was assembled as I hung the Hall of Fame medal around his neck for his service, all those years ago, as a lifeguard. I couldn't resist a joke, so I said, "Mr. President, you must realize that the real significance of this medal is that it proves that all jocks aren't necessarily jerks." He laughed, then promptly told us two or three stories of his days as a lifeguard.

More recently, I became chairman of the board of the John Douglas French Alzheimer Research Foundation at about the time, coincidentally, when Ron announced to the country that he was afflicted with this tragic ailment. The foundation raises funds for research. The foundation gave Nancy its distinguished medal several months ago. She made some beautiful remarks and I was happy I had a chance to be part of the family at this difficult time. Helping others becomes a very important part of one's life when you get to my age.

MIKE MANSFIELD

AMBASSADOR TO JAPAN, 1977–89;
SENATE MAJORITY LEADER 1961–77

"I received a call from him at two o'clock one morning."

Mike Mansfield was the longest-serving U.S. ambassador to Japan. Before that, he was the longest-serving U.S. Senate majority leader. A Democrat, he was first elected to the Senate from Montana in 1953. He served in the House of Representatives from 1943 to 1953. Prior to his public service, he was a professor of history and political science at the University of Montana. Today, he is the senior adviser for East Asia affairs at a major investment banking firm.

Ronald Reagan and I first met in Tokyo. As I recall, it was early 1978 and he was there to meet with political and business leaders before going on to Taiwan. He let me know he would be staying at the Hotel Okura, across the street from our embassy. I called on him and Mrs. Reagan and their party at the hotel the day they arrived. I found him outgoing and easy to talk with. What's more, I found we agreed on various matters involving U.S.-Japan relations. I invited them to a reception at the embassy the next day.

Later, after he had been elected President, I received a call from him at two o'clock one morning. I remember the time because I'm usually asleep at that hour and was surprised at such an early call. He asked me if I would like to stay on as ambassador to Japan. I told him I had my things packed already because, knowing politics, I figured my time was up and I was prepared to go home. After all, I had been appointed by his predecessor, Jimmy Carter. "Well," he said, "I'd like you to stay on and continue to serve." I said I would be delighted to. I appreciated it personally and did the best I could during the eight years I served under him.

During those years, President Reagan came over several times. He made a big hit with the Japanese people. As I look back on those years, I am convinced more and more that of all the recent administrations, his was the one that truly understood the importance of Japan, East Asia, and the Pacific. And his secretary of state, George Shultz, was the only secretary of state in recent memory who showed a similar personal interest in that part of the world.

I was honored to receive, along with George Shultz, the Presidential Medal of Freedom on President Reagan's last day in office. He had asked me to receive it the previous November, but because of the illness of the emperor of Japan I felt I couldn't leave at the time. The invitation was forthcoming again and I was delighted to be able to accept the honor.

I like Ronald Reagan very much personally. He is a man who has always been open, and there is nothing underhanded about him. Reagan always tried to be Reagan—and was until he was undercut by some of his subordinates who should have known better and acted more responsibly. I have in mind the Iran-Contra matter. They placed themselves above the good of the country and certainly ahead of the President who appointed them, and they took advantage of his openness.

He was certainly popular with the Japanese and had an instinctive liking for them. He was eager to learn about them. And, the feeling was mutual. I have not seen him since he left office, but I think he exited from public life most gracefully. I was sorry to hear about his affliction with Alzheimer's disease, but I know he is up to it, as one would expect him to be. And, he is so lucky to have such a devoted and loving wife.

EUGENE MCCARTHY
AUTHOR, FORMER U.S. SENATOR, AND
PRESIDENTIAL CANDIDATE

"He used colorful examples to illustrate his points."

Eugene McCarthy represented Minnesota in the U.S. Senate from 1959 to 1970. Before that, he was a member of the House of Representatives from 1946 to 1959, but he is most famous for his anti-Vietnam War candidacy for the Democratic presidential nomination in 1968. Supported by legions of enthusiastic young campaign workers, he had such a strong showing in the New Hampshire primary that year that President Lyndon Johnson soon announced he would not stand for reelection. Since retiring from the Senate, he has been a syndicated columnist, lecturer, and board member of a major publishing company. He is the author of many books, the latest of which is A Colony of the World *(1993).*

Ronald Reagan and I first met in the summer of 1975. It was at a luncheon meeting of business executives in New Jersey that had been billed as a debate, but really wasn't. He gave a kind of preview of what his campaign for President would be about. He asked to go first, and that was all right with me. I remember especially that he used colorful examples to illustrate his points. For example, when he talked about the unemployed, he said that if they held hands they would reach from New Jersey to San Diego. He was quite particular about that. Then he talked about the national debt and I recall him saying that if the dollar bills representing the total debt were stitched end-to-end they would reach the moon and back two or three times. The audience seemed quite taken by his examples.

I talked about general economic theory instead. When it was his turn to respond, there was no rebuttal to what I had said. He used the time to give another example of government excess. This time I think it was that famous "welfare queen" of Chicago—the woman who allegedly drew pension checks from several deceased husbands and owned several cars. He gave these anecdotal examples and I talked theory, so we never really met in debate. He was very personable, very affable. I just wasn't prepared to agree that the national debt would reach the moon and back!

Later, in the 1980 campaign, I endorsed him. There was no quid pro quo. I issued a statement to the effect that Ronald Reagan would be more likely than Jimmy Carter to do something about nuclear weapons. (I was glad that turned out to be true.) I also mentioned the high rates of inflation and interest under Carter and thought that Reagan would be more fiscally responsible. That proved true, also.

EDWIN MEESE III

U.S. ATTORNEY GENERAL, COUNSELOR TO THE
PRESIDENT, CHIEF OF STAFF TO THE GOVERNOR

"He was nearly always working."

Ed Meese served as attorney general of the United States from 1985 to 1988. Before that, he was counselor to the President from the beginning of Ronald Reagan's first term in 1981 (he was part of the troika that also included Chief of Staff James Baker and Deputy Chief of Staff Michael Deaver). As counselor, he served as the President's chief policy adviser. In Sacramento, he had served as Governor Reagan's chief of staff from 1969 to 1974. Prior to that, he was legal affairs secretary in the Governor's Office, and before that he was a deputy district attorney in Alameda County, California. In the late 1970s, he was a professor of law at the University of San Diego. A native Californian, he holds a bachelor's degree from Yale University and a law degree from Boalt Hall School of Law at the University of California, Berkeley. He currently holds the Ronald Reagan Chair of Public Policy at the Heritage Foundation in Washington, D.C., and is a distinguished visiting fellow at the Hoover Institution at Stanford University.

Ronald Reagan has an ability to inspire and attract personal loyalty from people like no one else I have ever met. He, in turn, gives his friendship, but he doesn't give it in varying degrees to different people. He is as friendly and outgoing to a relative stranger who he feels needs help as he would be to someone who has known him for a long time. Another important thing about him is that he doesn't have the usual ego needs you see in a lot of people in politics. I think he satisfied that during his movie career. As a consequence, he doesn't need to be surrounded by a group of camp followers.

I remember my first meeting with him, in late 1966. He had just been elected governor of California, but hadn't yet taken office. I had been asked to meet him, with the possibility of his offering me the position that was then called the executive clemency and extradition secretary in the Governor's Office (it later became legal affairs secretary). I was a lawyer and, at the time, was in the District Attorney's Office in Alameda County in Oakland. After a couple of meetings with his staff, I had come to talk with him in person. I had never met him before.

We talked about law enforcement and crime control, the things I had spent the last ten years working on. I was amazed at how much information he could assimilate and respond to, adding his own ideas. He seemed to know as much about these subjects as I did. After a while, he offered me the job and I accepted on the spot. I drove home and told my wife we were moving to Sacramento. There wasn't a doubt in my mind that this was the man I wanted to work for.

Another thing happened in those early days that illustrates his capacity to absorb information, understand it, then utilize it. I'd been on the job perhaps two weeks. He was to have his first meeting with law enforcement leaders—several police chiefs and sheriffs. I had carefully worked over a one- or two-page memo for him that gave him an outline of things he might discuss with this group. I took the memo in to him a few minutes before the meeting, thinking he would use it as a talking paper. He read it over once, laid it on his desk, and walked down the hall to the meeting. He addressed the group for about fifteen minutes, using all the ideas in my memo and adding his own—as if he had been preparing for that meeting for several weeks!

In that same room, I recall he held a meeting with a group of student body presidents and leaders from colleges around the state. This was at a time when there was a lot of unrest because of the war in Vietnam. We had that issue to deal with, along with such things as whether the University of California should charge tuition. Governor Reagan, as an ex officio member of the university's board of regents and the board of trustees of the California State University and College system, was right in the middle of it all. He was determined to restore and keep order on the campuses and to increase the quality of education in the state. He was particularly concerned about some of the ultraliberal faculty members who were actually impeding learning on the campuses.

In the middle of this meeting, one of the student body presidents said, "Governor, you just can't understand our generation. When you were our age, you didn't have intercontinental air travel as we have today, or television or instantaneous communication around the globe." Ronald Reagan said, "No, my generation didn't have those things; we invented them." He understood these young people and how to be relevant to them.

As a leader, his ability to communicate was especially important in times of adversity. When the space shuttle *Challenger* was lost, in 1987, his immediate response was to try to calm people and have them reflect on the bigger picture; his aim was not to eliminate grief, but to direct it toward the ultimate healing process. The speech he gave, about reaching out to touch the hand of God, showed his ability to empathize with those who suffered.

People call him the Great Communicator, but his ability didn't lie just in his delivery of a speech. Rather, it was based on his interest in people—their needs and thoughts—and his response to that. Although he was the only one talking, in many ways it was as if he were having a conversation with his audience. His success was a combination of his understanding of people and his desire to get his message across as one that was meant for them.

I think that this came from his roots. He was from the heartland of America, growing up in a small town, with its customs and mores and sense of community. He has never lost that. In fact, that was his frame of reference for what America is all about. So, he could address the farmer, the grocer, the storekeeper. (He knew about the storekeeper firsthand, because his father had been one. And he had known adversity, for his father had some bitter business reverses.)

During World War II, while he didn't go overseas, he did serve and was deeply interested in all aspects of the conflict. One of the things he used to do, as adjutant of the training film squadron in the Army Air Corps, was read the narratives of Congressional Medal of Honor winners that would come across his desk. He was deeply affected by these accounts of heroism and bravery, for here again, he thought these traits were part of what America was about.

He had volunteered for the Army Reserve in the mid-1930s. That was when he was a radio announcer in Des Moines, Iowa. He really wanted to ride horses and the only way he could figure out to do it, since he had very little money, was to join the Cavalry Reserve at Fort Des Moines. He enlisted, then took the exams to become a second lieutenant. When World War II came, he was called up as an officer. But in his preinduction physical exam, they found that his eyesight was so bad (he had always worn glasses) that he could not be assigned to combat duty. At first, he was assigned to the Port of Embarkation at Fort Mason, San Francisco; then he was transferred to the training film unit in Los Angeles.

Late in his second term as President, he had the most difficult experience of his public life, the Iran-Contra issue. The initiative toward Iran was intended to cultivate communication with moderate elements within that strategically important country—and there were some. Our allies and we were concerned about Iran, not only because it was in the hands of the Ayatollah Khomeini and his followers, but also because of the uncertainty that might follow his death. It was an important country because it was next door to the Soviet Union and the Soviets always had their eye on influencing or perhaps controlling Iran. It was also important because we wanted to diminish Iranian state-sponsored terrorism. By establishing some level of communication, we frankly hoped to get these elements to influence the groups in Lebanon that had taken Americans as hostages. We wanted to locate the hostages and get them home. It was a very complex thing.

At the same time, President Reagan was committed to supporting the freedom fighters in Nicaragua. When these two issues were brought together, it was like a match and a fuse coming in contact. Some of the President's opponents in Congress opposed him on one of these issues and some on the other. They now came together.

The two missions were marred by a very unfortunate misjudgment on the part of some overzealous people who decided to divert funds from one project to the other.

The President had several reactions. One was to preserve both missions. He considered both important to our national security, but the freedom fighters were the more important of the two. Second, he was torn because he realized these initiatives had been jeopardized by people who thought they were doing things to help him accomplish the mission, even though they were the wrong things to do. At the same time, he could not allow this problem to keep him from continuing with the basic thrust of his administration: strengthening the economy and working to bring the cold war to an end.

I do not think his having to cope with this all at once undermined his basic optimism. There was talk at the time that he was depressed by Iran-Contra. I didn't find it to be so. In fact, I talked with him one day in December 1986. It was just the two of us and, as we were walking out of the Oval Office, I said, "Mr. President, I hope this isn't getting you down—all these problems with Iran-Contra." He said, "No, Ed, I don't have to worry. Nancy worries enough for both of us." That was his way of letting me know that he was okay, even though it was a difficult task to cope with Congress under the circumstances.

The two missions had been intended to be totally separate, both as to geography and execution. It just happened that a cou-

ple of people on the National Security Council staff had responsibilities in both areas. That's where the opportunity arose to
divert the monies that were received from the sale of a small
amount of defensive weapons to the moderate Iranians. Those
monies were diverted to the program of support for the Nicar-
aguan freedom fighters.

One thing about Ronald Reagan that has particularly impressed me over the thirty years I have known him is that he was
nearly always working. He has often been described by the press
as laid-back or even lazy. I never found that to be true. He would
work in the car as we went from, say, Sacramento to the San
Francisco Bay Area, or on an airplane going cross-country. He
was always reading and making notes or working on a speech. A
lot of the things he said publicly and a lot of the policies he
sponsored had been well thought out during these travel times.
He never dawdled or just did crossword puzzles as many people
do under such circumstances. He was using the time to prepare
himself.

His tremendous self-discipline was revealed in two ways. One
involved his determination to carefully study everything he
needed to in the evening, to be ready for the next day's schedule.
We had to be careful what we put in his "in" tray because he
considered anything there to be essential reading. And he set aside
time every evening to go over this material.

The other evidence of his self-discipline was the fact that he
may be the only President to have come out of the White House
physically stronger than he went in. At the time he was shot, in
March 1981, he had just finished campaigning for a year and had
not had a chance to get much exercise, which he missed. When
he'd been governor, he exercised regularly, including his
horseback riding.

When he was recovering from the gunshot wound, the doctors
said he should get back onto a regimen of exercise. So some gym
equipment, including a treadmill, was moved into the White
House. Virtually every night thereafter, he would exercise after
work while watching the nightly television news programs. It

was therapeutic and invigorating for him. As a result, he added to his chest size and biceps, but he did it as a means of self-discipline because he knew it was the right thing to do.

I think his self-discipline contributed to what appeared to be the ease with which he moved through every day. In baseball, they say, the greatest players make the hardest plays look easy. I think Ronald Reagan made both of his toughest jobs—governor and president—look easy because he was so good at them.

BRIAN MULRONEY
PRIME MINISTER OF CANADA, 1984—93

"He knew how the American people wanted a President to conduct himself, and that is exactly what he did."

The Right Honorable Brian Mulroney was elected to Canada's House of Commons in August 1983 and became the Leader of the Opposition that year. The following year, he led the Progressive Conservative party to the largest parliamentary victory in Canadian history. His government was reelected for a second mandate in 1988. He served until June 1993, when he resigned to return to private life as an attorney in Montreal.

He was born in Baie Comeau, Quebec, where he grew up as a bilingual Canadian. He earned his bachelor's degree from St. Francis Xavier University in Nova Scotia and his law degree from Laval University in Quebec City. He and his wife, Mila, have four children.

Mulroney and Ronald Reagan developed a close friendship and working relationship during their years as leaders of their respective countries. In 1988 they saw the U.S.-Canada Free Trade Agreement go into effect. It was the precursor to the North American Free Trade Agreement, which also included Mexico—a result Reagan had foreseen in 1979 when he announced his candidacy for President.

I remember the conclusion of a state visit by President Reagan to Ottawa. The closing ceremonies had been held and he and I drove to the airport with the Secret Service. We drove into a large, empty airplane hangar, where we were to meet our wives just before the official farewell and the Reagans' departure. He and I were standing there in this huge hangar when the other limo arrived and out stepped Nancy and my wife, Mila. They started to walk toward us. They both looked terrific. Reagan looked at both of them, put his arm around me, and said, "You know, Brian, for two Irishmen, we certainly married up." This was typical of that great sense of humor of his.

Another instance occurred at a state dinner at the White House. That dinner, in our honor, happened to be just before my birthday. He rose and said, "We are honored to have Prime Minister Mulroney and his wife, Mila, with us at the White House. They are a marvelous couple and Nancy and I have developed a very special relationship with them." Then he added, "Tomorrow the prime minister is going to be forty-nine. What can I say when the head of a government is going to be forty-nine years of age except, 'Good luck, kid.' "

Ronald Reagan had a great serenity about him. Coming to office at age seventy as he did, he had none of the questions that often torment young leaders. He came with the full assurance of the value of his ideas and he didn't clutter up his mind or his administration by proposing a thousand new ones. He had five or six fundamentals, which he believed, and he pursued them relentlessly. He understood what the French call *la notion de l'état,* a sense of statehood. He had an instinctive understanding of how important that was to the people of the United States. He always conducted himself accordingly. He never trivialized the presidency, and he understood both the substance and symbols of government.

Ronald Reagan and I became fast friends. I watched him over the years and he never wavered. He pursued his goals through the economic summits of the G-7 nations, sometimes through the United Nations, sometimes bilaterally, and sometimes unilaterally. The free trade agreement between Canada and the United States has resulted in the largest trade between any two nations in the world. Our long-range objective was free trade throughout the hemisphere, something he had been speaking of for years.

I came to know and value him as a loyal friend and colleague and a delightful fellow-Celt with a happy Irish heart and a very generous view of the world. He always conducted himself with a great amount of courtesy. I never saw him be rude to anyone, though some were rude to him. I never saw him react in anger at a high-level meeting, nor did he ever throw his weight around. He always spoke softly. It goes back to *la notion de l'état*. He knew how the American people wanted a President to conduct himself, and that is exactly what he did.

LYN NOFZIGER
POLITICAL AND COMMUNICATIONS ADVISER

"We broke out the champagne."

Lyn Nofziger spent the first half of his career as a journalist and was Washington correspondent for Copley Newspapers and the Copley News Service. In 1966, he became press secretary in Ronald Reagan's successful campaign for the governorship of California. He then became director of communications in the new Reagan administration in Sacramento. In 1969, he joined the Nixon White House as Assistant to the President. In 1972, he managed Nixon's winning reelection campaign in California. He held senior positions in the 1976 Reagan for President campaign. From 1977 to 1979, he was executive vice chairman of Citizens for the Republic, then press secretary in the 1980 Reagan presidential campaign. In 1981, he became assistant to the President for political affairs in the Reagan White House. In 1984, he was a senior adviser to the Reagan-Bush reelection campaign. Since 1982, he has also headed a political and communications consultancy. A native of California, he has had four books published, his memoirs and three western novels.

My introduction to Ronald Reagan took place in 1965, before he had made up his mind to run for governor of California. It was in the town of Newark, Ohio. He came there to do a fund-raiser with Bill Buckley for Congressman John Ashbrook. The next day, he was to speak at a Salute to Ray Bliss, the Republican national chairman, in Cincinnati.

Near Newark, there was a cocktail party at a farm before the dinner and speech. I was a reporter in those days and I went out with an old friend whose family owned the *Columbus Dispatch*. We waited around for Reagan to appear. He was terribly late because in those days he would only travel by train. He had gone by train to Cincinnati, then by car up to Newark. He was so late to the cocktail party that everyone had left for the dinner except for two or three drunks and me—and I was gloriously drunk. I went up and introduced myself to him because I had known his brother Neil, nicknamed "Moon." Moon had been a television adviser to Barry Goldwater in the presidential campaign a year earlier, 1964, and I had covered it for Copley.

When Ronald Reagan saw that I was less than sober, he quickly excused himself. I covered his after-dinner speech that night, but couldn't read my notes so I never wrote a story.

A month or so later, when I was scheduled to go to California, I called Neil and said that everyone expected his brother to run for governor and could I interview him? Moon set up a lunch for me with Ron and himself at the Brown Derby, just off Hollywood and Vine. I got there about noon and Ron came in about fifteen minutes late. I stood up and said, "My name is Lyn Nofziger. You may not remember, but we met before." He said, "Oh, yes I do!"—so I changed the subject. It was an interesting lunch. He was quite affable, but he was also good—even at that early time—at not saying anything he didn't want to say. He refused to say that he was going to run; only that he was "looking at it" and would make up his mind. So, that was my real introduction to Ronald Reagan.

A few months later, I was surprised when Stu Spencer called and asked me to be Reagan's press secretary in the 1966 gubernatorial campaign. I said I had a good job and didn't want to do it. They finally called Jim Copley, the head of Copley Newspapers. He asked me to do it just until the primary, possibly thinking Reagan would be all through by then. I accepted.

Wherever he went, I went with him. It was mostly in the back of a car, because he was still a white-knuckle flier. A turkey rancher in Stockton had an old DC-3 he used to ferry turkey chicks to his customers. He offered to lend it to the campaign. We put some seats in it and called it *The Turkey Gobbler*. We traveled up and down California in that airplane unless we were in a real hurry, in which case we'd take a commercial flight.

Reagan was determined to prove he was up to this campaign. His managers, Stu Spencer and Bill Roberts, didn't have a lot of faith in him. Like Pat Brown, the incumbent, they thought of him as "just an actor." He was determined to prove he wasn't. So, much against the inclination of his campaign managers, he began taking questions at all his speaking events.

Everything went well, with a few exceptions. One of those took place in northwestern California. Somebody in the crowd asked him, "What are you going to do about the Eel River project?" He said, "Where's the Eel River?" The man answered, "You're standing on it." This was unfortunate because it wasn't Ronald Reagan's fault; his staff had not given him the proper briefing. We made sure it didn't happen again.

Thinking about his presidential campaigns, I recall that he wasn't sure until late 1975 that he wanted to run against a sitting president for the 1976 nomination. When he did run, it turned out to be uphill all the way. I think one big thing that probably cost him the nomination was a speech he made in Chicago in September 1975—the so-called Ninety-Billion-Dollar speech— in which he said $90 billion could be cut from the federal budget. It was not the speech that caused him trouble, but the addendum, a list of actual programs and dollars that could be cut. The press didn't pay much attention to the speech or the addendum at the time, but Stu Spencer, who was then working for the Gerald Ford campaign, got a copy of it and just lay in the weeds for us, so to speak.

By the time we got to the New Hampshire primary, Stu had primed the press and local Ford supporters with plenty of questions, such as, "Do we have to have a state income tax?" and so forth. With a long list of oxen that might be gored, thanks to that speech addendum, people had doubts about Reagan and enough of these stuck to deprive him of a victory.

The other mistake, regarding New Hampshire, was when Hugh Gregg, a former governor and our state chairman, told Reagan to take off the weekend before election day. We did, and campaigned in the mud in Illinois. But Ford stayed in New Hampshire. Thus, it looked as if Ford cared and Reagan didn't. We lost by a narrow margin and from there we went from one loss to another.

At one point, I dropped off for a couple of days to go to our national headquarters in Washington, then met the campaign in North Carolina, where Reagan was making his last visit. On his arrival there that morning, we learned that a number of senior elected Republicans were calling for Reagan to drop out. So when he got off the plane, all the reporters chimed in, asking him when he was going to do so. He dug in his heels that day. Paul Laxalt, his chairman, was along and told him to put away his speech cards (those four-by-six-inch cards on which he wrote his notes) and just speak from the heart. He did, and he insisted to all of us he was not getting out of the race. "We're going all the way to Texas" (a primary several weeks away that we were sure we would win), he declared.

From North Carolina we flew to La Crosse, Wisconsin. That evening, as Reagan was speaking at a Ducks Unlimited dinner, the late Frank Reynolds, ABC's news anchor, came up to us and said, "You may not believe this, but you guys are winning in North Carolina." Reagan, always a bit superstitious, did not want to talk with the press after the dinner to claim victory, in case the figures coming out of North Carolina were incomplete and changed. So we all got on the plane, headed for Los Angeles. Not long after we were airborne, the pilot announced that with more than 90 percent of the votes counted, we had won. We broke out the champagne—and the gin.

That was in late March. While we'd finally won our first primary, the campaign was broke. So John Sears, the campaign manager, did what he had to do. He canceled most of Reagan's April appearances and scheduled a half-hour nationally televised fundraising speech by Reagan. The idea was to leapfrog the primaries and appeal to Reagan's national constituency. After some effort, we managed to raise the money to put the speech on the air. It was vintage Reagan. He was at his best and the results were spectacular.

The money rolled in, and in, and in. We couldn't spend it all, as things turned out. So, several months later, after the campaign was over and all the accounting had been done, we had a surplus. I proposed that it be used to create Citizens for the Republic (CFTR), with Ronald Reagan as chairman. It would be a political action committee (PAC) that could support a number of candidates. It opened for business in early 1977. We put on a series of nuts-and-bolts campaign seminars for volunteers all over the country, usually with Reagan as the keynote speaker. A lot of the folks who came to these events ended up working in the 1980 Reagan campaign. And, meanwhile, we were supporting candidates for various offices who shared his philosophy.

ROBERT NOVAK
COLUMNIST, TELEVISION COMMENTATOR,
NEWSLETTER EDITOR

"He was not obsessed with politics."

Following his college years at the University of Illinois and two years of active duty as an Army officer during the Korean War, Robert Novak became a reporter for the Associated Press in Omaha, Nebraska. He later joined the Washington bureau of The Wall Street Journal. *In 1963, he teamed up with Rowland Evans to write "Inside Report" a nationally syndicated column. In 1993, Mr. Evans retired from the column and Bob Novak continues to write it three times a week. He and Mr. Evans produce a biweekly newsletter,* The Evans-Novak Political Report, *and an interview program on CNN. He is also seen regularly on CNN's* Capital Gang *and* Crossfire. *He is the author of several books and is a roving editor of* Reader's Digest.

When Ronald Reagan didn't want to talk politics or issues with reporters, he had ways of avoiding these things without irritating them. I remember one time in 1975, when he was testing the waters for the 1976 presidential nomination. I met him in Jackson, Mississippi, to follow along to his next event, a trade association convention speech in Boca Raton, Florida. We were in a small airplane, just four of us including the pilot. There were some terrible thunderstorms that night, so a flight that would normally have taken two hours took us four hours to fly around the worst parts. I settled in, thinking we'd have a wonderful discussion, but he he didn't want to talk politics, so he told Hollywood stories. It was a delightful time, but every time I tried to get back to politics, he would move away from the subject.

I recall that a similar thing happened when he was in the White House, at a luncheon during his second term. The format was to gather together two or three journalists, Don Regan, who was then chief of staff, Pat Buchanan, who was the communications director, and the President. It was around the time they were trying to get Ferdinand Marcos to step aside in the Philippines. Each of us journalists was trying to get Reagan to say something about the issue, but the matter was at a delicate stage and he didn't want to talk about it. Rather than conceding that, he said, "You know, one thing I tried to do but was never successful at was to get them to make a movie about the Philippine Scouts. Do you know about them? They were Filipino troops who were heroic in the defense of Bataan and then became guerrilla fighters." He went on to describe the plot of the movie that was never made. All this took about fifteen minutes out of the hour we were to have with him. He just ran out the clock.

Another thing I recall from that luncheon was a question I asked him about the gold standard. I was a great fan of it and I was sure that, in his heart, he was, too. But, when I asked about it, he said, "Well"—and he looked over at Regan—"Don won't let me."

I first met Ronald Reagan in Cincinnati in 1965. A lot of reporters had gone out to see him. He had a press conference scheduled. It was hot, and all the reporters were a little disheveled. He came in right after a series of events and had a fundraising speech to give that night. He wore a blue blazer and gray trousers. He looked like a million bucks and twenty years younger than he actually was. We had a laugh when, after a while, he excused himself, saying he had to "freshen up."

That night he gave a terrific speech and I wrote a column about him being the Republican answer to John F. Kennedy, who had been gone about a year and a half then. I wasn't the only one making the comparison, but Mary McGrory called me to say that it was outrageous, sacrilegious, and profane to compare "this movie actor" to JFK.

After he was elected governor of California, I had numerous interviews with him and did an article on him for *The Saturday Evening Post*. His daughter Maureen invited me to brunch one time at their home. He was always very cordial, but he couldn't seem to remember my name. It wasn't until *The McLaughlin Group* went on the air in 1982—and I was part of the program initially—that he began to call me by name.

One of his great strengths, to my mind, is that he was not obsessed with politics. For example, he went to eight Gridiron Club dinners. Nixon and Carter hated going to them, but Reagan loved them. He really enjoyed the show; the satirical skits. He sat next to eight different Gridiron presidents at those dinners—remember they're all working journalists—and they all tried to get him to talk about the issues of the days, but he wouldn't do it.

He was way ahead of his time in many ways. Back in 1975, he made a speech in Chicago that he caught hell for, about turning back many government functions—and the revenue to pay for them—to the states. Well, that's happening now and it's what's going to happen in the future.

One thing that always impressed me about Reagan: He didn't bear grudges against people who had been his adversaries. For example, Stu Spencer, who had been his gubernatorial campaign manager in 1966 in California, went to work for Ford in 1976 and used elements of that Chicago speech to undermine the Reagan campaign in New Hampshire. It contributed to Reagan's defeat there, yet, in 1980, Stu was back on the Reagan team and bygones were bygones.

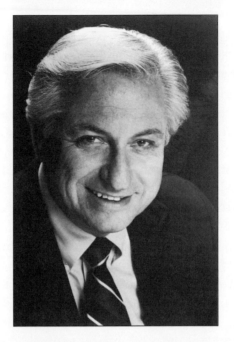

HARRY O'CONNOR
REAGAN RADIO PROGRAM PRODUCER

"He loves people and likes to interact with them."

Harry O'Connor left a successful broadcasting career in Texas in 1964 to join cartoon voice expert Mel Blanc ("Bugs Bunny" and others) in Los Angeles as a comedy writer and producer. Later that decade he launched his own firm, O'Connor Creative Services, which became one of the nation's leading producers and syndicators of radio features. In early 1975, shortly after Ronald Reagan completed his second term as governor of California and was once again a private citizen, O'Connor launched his five-day-a-week commentary program. These five-minute "issues vignettes" became widely successful over the nearly five years they were on the air. At its peak, the series was carried by more than 350 radio stations and heard by an estimated 10 million listeners each week.

We produced the Reagan program every third Thursday—recording three weeks' worth at a sitting. His recording schedule was locked in months in advance. Anything else that came up had to be scheduled around that, which indicated the importance he and his staff attached to the project. He would always arrive early and in a good mood, with time to chat, tell a story or two, and put everyone at ease before he stepped into the recording booth. He was always fully prepared, with fifteen scripts, each about three minutes in length.

He drafted many of the scripts himself. In other cases, his staff would do the first drafts and he'd rework them for better sound patterns. His early radio training meant that he wrote for the ear, not the eye, and that was an advantage.

Now and then there would be a recording glitch. Typical of Ronald Reagan—and untypical of many people when they record—if he blew a line or some words were missing in the script, when we stopped to make the correction, he would say, "Well, I messed up again." It was never, "Darn those secretaries, they can never get anything right," or blaming some other staffer.

Occasionally, Nancy would join him at the studio, particularly after we had moved to North Hollywood. She would wait in the office while we recorded. She was always wonderful to visit with.

Our North Hollywood studios were on a floor of a high-rise bank building, down a long hallway from the elevators, with several other firms in between, including a direct mail company. One day, my office manager came in just as we were finishing a Reagan recording session. She had a birthday card in her hand and asked me if it would be all right for her to have Governor Reagan sign it. It was for the receptionist at the direct mail company. I took the card into him and he asked where she worked. I said it was just down the hall. "Let's go and say 'hello,' " he said, so we did. As he walked in the door, the receptionist's mouth dropped open. "I understand it's your birthday today," he said. She was speechless, but nodded. He then asked her if he could sign "Happy Birthday" to her, and did. Several dozen office workers had gathered around and the applause rang out when he finished. He shook hands all around. This is Reagan! He loves people and likes to interact with them.

We had many good times at those sessions. At his very first one, in Hollywood in early 1975, I had invited some old friends to be there to greet him: Art Linkletter, Jack Webb, Efrem Zimbalist, Jr., Ralph Storey, and John Carradine. And in August 1976, when he resumed his radio program after losing the Republican nomination to Gerald Ford in Kansas City, for his first new recording session, Sally Cobb, widow of Bob Cobb, who created the Brown Derby restaurants, came over with champagne and strawberries, silver, crystal, two waiters—the works, from the Derby next door.

Those radio commentaries were the inspiration for Ronald Reagan's weekly live broadcasts when he became President. Mike Deaver proposed the idea so that the people could hear Reagan speak live. The idea was that he would do it every Saturday and any station could pick it up. Initially, the Mutual Broadcasting System carried it. Several other people on the White House staff thought it wouldn't work, but Reagan liked it and did it. A side benefit was that Sunday newspapers would carry stories based on the Saturday radio commentary. What Ronald Reagan started has now become a tradition. Both Presidents Bush and Clinton have carried on the weekly broadcast and the political opposition has a chance to do its own broadcast, too.

After Ronald Reagan became President, he appointed me to the board of the Corporation for Public Broadcasting. It came as a surprise to me and was a great honor. It turned out I was the only one around who hadn't lobbied to get on the board!

Back when I was first getting into broadcasting I was told that one of the best sources for learning about announcing was a Dr. Palmer, who owned a chiropractic college in Davenport, Iowa, along with radio stations WOC there and WHO in Des Moines. Most of what "Doc" Palmer wrote made sense, although it didn't help me lose my Texas accent (I still say we're "awn" the radio instead of "on"). He was a zealot about being concise. He didn't like the word "the" used. He said you shouldn't state anything that was obvious to the listener and you should get right to the point. Also, he warned against using negatives. Little did I know at the time that Ronald Reagan had begun his career working for Doc Palmer on those two stations. Doc's star pupil took to communication naturally.

SANDRA DAY O'CONNOR

ASSOCIATE JUSTICE OF THE SUPREME COURT OF THE UNITED STATES

"I was overwhelmed."

At the time Sandra Day O'Connor was nominated by President Reagan to be the first woman justice of the Supreme Court, in July 1981, she was serving on the Arizona Court of Appeals. Before that she had been a superior court judge in Maricopa County, Arizona, from 1975 to 1979. Prior to that, she was a member of the state senate from 1969 to 1975 (elected majority leader in 1972). Earlier she served as an assistant attorney general, state of Arizona. She holds bachelor's and law degrees from Stanford University.

Ronald Reagan and I first met in Phoenix in the early 1970s. He was governor then. He had come to speak at a dinner of the Trunk and Tusk, an Arizona Republican group. That was in the early seventies. I had been involved as a state legislator, working on a constitutional amendment to link state spending increases to certain increases in the income of the people. Governor Reagan had been working on a similar proposal in California, Proposition One. I had an opportunity to shake his hand and to mention this project, but it was not until 1981 that we met again.

That summer, Attorney General William French Smith telephoned to ask me to come to Washington, D.C., to talk to various people in connection with the vacancy on the Supreme Court, caused by the retirement of Justice Potter Stewart. I met with Attorney General Smith and several members of the White House staff. Then the attorney general asked me to meet with the President.

I was combining these visits with a meeting in Washington of a private organization on whose board I sat, and this group was meeting in a building near DuPont Circle. I told the attorney general I would be happy to come, but I had never been to the White House and didn't know where to go or how to get in. He said he would ask his secretary to pick me up. The next thing I knew, I was being conducted toward the Oval Office. We stopped on the way at the small office next to it that was occupied by Mike Deaver. He and I chatted; then I was escorted in to meet with the President.

That was my first glimpse of not only the Oval Office, but the White House as well, and it was almost too much to take in all at once. President Reagan was there, with Attorney General Smith and a number of the staff members I had met the previous day. He invited us all to be seated and chatted pleasantly about my ranch background and his interest in ranching and horseback riding. He was warm and friendly and put me immediately at ease. We then discussed more substantive issues and had a fine conversation. It was clear that, despite a twinkle in his eye and the ability to tell an anecdote and share a laugh, he was a man who knew where he was headed and what he wanted to discuss.

I left Washington for Arizona that afternoon, reflecting on the flight back what a marvelous experience it had been. Still, I felt sure I would not be asked to take the job. They had been interviewing other people and I was thrilled to be part of the process.

I knew he was looking for a woman, but since there was already an Arizonan on the court—William Rehnquist (we had been in the same class in law school)—I thought they would look elsewhere. On reflection, it seemed unlikely that he would have two on the Court from a state the size of Arizona, and especially two with such similar legal educational backgrounds. Nevertheless, I talked it over with my husband and he encouraged me to accept if it were offered. I had more qualms about it than he did.

I was very surprised when, about a week later, the telephone rang in my chambers at the Arizona Court of Appeals and it was the White House calling. President Reagan came on the line and he said he would like to announce my nomination to the Supreme Court the next morning. I was overwhelmed and, at first, speechless. After a moment, I managed to tell him that I would be honored. He said the White House would send someone from the press office to be with me the next day when the announcement was made. I was unprepared for the furor that occurred when it was made. I didn't see it on television, but soon saw the droves of reporters and cameras around our house, the court, and all over Phoenix.

After my confirmation by the Senate, I was sworn in one day in late September 1981. President Reagan had decided I should come to the White House with my family and we would go together to the Supreme Court building on Capitol Hill, where he would present me for the swearing-in ceremony. It was highly symbolic, for most Supreme Court justices these days are sworn in at the White House. His gesture showed he had great respect for the third branch of government and was going to show it by coming to the Court. In the Court room, he didn't have a word to say! The ceremony is very brief and there is no role in it for the President. He and Mrs. Reagan sat in the front row, looking on. For me it was a glorious occasion, and the President exhibited a great deal of happiness in his appointing me.

During President Reagan's terms, my husband and I were invited to the White House on several occasions. The President also decided to reinstate an old custom: Once a year, all the justices of the Court would be invited to the White House to meet with the President. There would be a small reception for us, or a luncheon. The last such event was for both active and retired justices and was a luncheon. When we got there, it was clear something was going on. There was a delay and we awaited his arrival for some time in a reception room. Finally, we were told there was some news concerning the Iran-Contra issue and, as it turned out, that was the very moment the news broke. Belatedly, we went into the State dining room for lunch with the President. I sat opposite him. Ed Meese was then the attorney general and told us some of what had been said that day about the issue. It was amazing news to us, but the President looked relaxed. He and Justice Thurgood Marshall each told a few funny stories over lunch; then it was back to the Court for us.

President Reagan was always gracious and warm to my husband and me. We treasured the moments we had with this remarkable man.

VERNE ORR
SECRETARY OF THE AIR FORCE;
CALIFORNIA DIRECTOR OF FINANCE

"I think he'll be judged fairly, probably as one of the
best Presidents of the twentieth century."

Verne Orr, like many of his colleagues in Ronald Reagan's Sacramento and Wash-
ington administrations, left a successful business career for public service. In 1967,
in Sacramento, he became the new administration's first director of the Department
of Motor Vehicles. From 1970 until the end of Ronald Reagan's second term as
governor, he headed the state's Department of Finance. In 1980, he was deputy
director of the Reagan-Carter transition, then was appointed by President Reagan
as secretary of the Air Force, where he served longer than any of his predecessors,
five years, from 1981 to 1985. Today, "retired," he is back in Pasadena, Cal-
ifornia, where he is studying for a doctoral degree.

As a manager, Ronald Reagan did not like controversy or
discord among his people. In Sacramento, for example, Ed

Meese, as chief of staff, tried to see that disputes between, say, cabinet members or agency heads were settled outside the Governor's Office. In the five years I served as finance director, Reagan was careful to back me on every occasion, with one exception, because to overrule the finance director was to invite trouble. As soon as people knew they could go over his head and get a reversal, the line formed to the right.

Soon after I joined his cabinet, I learned his body English. I knew from it that sometimes he wasn't too happy with supporting my position. When that was the case, he would lay his glasses down on the table, shift in that straight chair he always used, and say, "Have you considered this very carefully, Verne?" I would underscore the reasons for my position and he would support it. But I knew when he was not altogether happy about it. So, when that occurred, I'd think it over and, two or three days later, I'd go back to him and say, "Governor, I think we may be able to find the money to give so-and-so about eighty percent of what they are asking." He would beam. So, I would call the department head and say, "I talked to the governor and we've been able to find a little more money." So when you worked for him, you learned to make him comfortable without compromising your principles. You recognized that he was the boss, that he wanted the decision to go a certain way, but didn't want to get the result by overruling his people. That's why learning his body English was so important.

One small but significant example of that body English occurred during his Washington years. If you were to study video clips of his first months as President, when he walked toward his helicopter and would get a salute from the honor guard, he would wave his hand, at about waist level. Gradually, that wave went higher and higher. One day he asked if it would be appropriate for a civilian—himself—to return a salute. I consider a salute a token of respect, like a handshake, so I said, if you're comfortable and want to do it, that's fine. He worked at it, gradually, and I felt the service men and women appreciated it. In the later years, his salute was really quite snappy.

I think President Reagan will be judged fairly, probably as one of the best Presidents of the twentieth century. As Martin Anderson says, he led a revolution in the way we think and act about our government. It would not have occurred without him. He began to turn government around and now, all these years later, we are into what might be called the second installment of that revolution.

KATHY OSBORNE

SECRETARY/ASSISTANT TO RONALD REAGAN AS
GOVERNOR, PRESIDENT, AND FORMER PRESIDENT

"I don't think anything affected him more deeply than this."

Reared and schooled in California, Kathleen Osborne joined the gubernatorial staff in Sacramento, first as assistant personal secretary to Governor Reagan in 1969, then as personal secretary to First Lady Nancy Reagan. After that, she was a businesswoman, owning a dress boutique in Sacramento until joining the White House staff as personal secretary to the President in 1981. In 1985, she became a special assistant to the President; in 1987 a deputy assistant; and in 1988, an assistant to the President. She was Mr. Reagan's executive assistant in his post-presidential office in Los Angeles from January 1989 through June 1991.

Thinking back to President Reagan's first term in the White House, it seemed for a time as if there were back-to-back hijackings and hostage-takings. He would focus on these problems intensely, but if we then had someone coming in to be honored, he would put the crisis aside for the moment, smile, and treat the visitor as if he or she were the most important person in the world. One of the things people would often express to me after such meetings with him was, "I couldn't tell you a thing that was in that room. All I saw was him!" After such meetings, he would again turn to the crisis at hand.

I can remember only one time when he had trouble doing this (when you're going in and out of his office ten to twenty times a day, you get to know his moods). He was almost always in a good mood, but this one time I could tell he was not concentrating on what was going on in the meeting because he had just learned that Mrs. Reagan was going to have surgery. (She was to have this about ten days later. She had put it off so she wouldn't have to cancel any of her appointments with her antidrug program. She put her duties as First Lady ahead of her personal well-being.) But, it was very difficult for the President, going through his daily schedule knowing she was facing this surgery and not knowing how serious it might be.

During those days and during Mrs. Reagan's recovery, we knew how much he wanted to be with her and, if his afternoon schedule was mostly staff meetings, I would call the chief of staff and say, "I think the boss needs to go home to be with Mrs. Reagan," and we would juggle the schedule so the President could have time to do this.

Only a few days after her surgery, her mother, Edie Davis, died. Elaine Crispen, Mrs. Reagan's press secretary, got word first, from a friend in Arizona who had been close to Mrs. Davis. She let me know, but the President had just started a live interview for European television. I decided to wait to tell him after the interview. Meanwhile, I called Mrs. Reagan's secretary and asked her to hold incoming calls, because I knew the President would want to tell her himself. I informed the chief of staff and he arranged to cancel the President's schedule for the rest of the day. I then told the President's aide Jim Kuhn to bring him to the President's private study next to the Oval Office immediately after the taping. Today, there wouldn't be time for his usual few minutes of visiting with the newspeople. I was waiting for him with some papers. He was surprised to see me there and sat down in front of the folders holding the papers. "I'm afraid I have some bad news for you. Mrs. Reagan's mother has died," I said. The news hit him hard because he adored Mrs. Davis as if she were his own mother. His first question was, "Does Nancy know?" "No, she doesn't," I replied. "I thought you would want to be the one to tell her." He said, "Of course; I need to." As he got up, he looked at the folders on the desk and asked if he needed to attend to them. "No. You go home to Mrs. Reagan. We've cleared your schedule."

I had called Dr. Hutton, the President's physician, who came over and walked home with the President to be with him when he told Mrs. Reagan. I think it must have been one of the hardest things President Reagan ever had to do, to tell his wife that her mother was gone. It was a lot for a man in his position. He wanted to be a strong, supportive husband and take care of everything; yet we all expected him to be our President and to take care of the whole world. In all the years I have known him, I don't think anything affected him more deeply than this.

The next day, the President took Mrs. Reagan, her secretary, and a small staff to Arizona for Mrs. Davis's memorial service. It was a very solemn trip. Mrs. Reagan, still recuperating from her surgery, stayed on in Phoenix to begin taking care of her mother's affairs. The President gave a beautiful eulogy at the service; then we returned to Washington.

It was suddenly all business again, getting ready for the Gorbachev summit. Things were happening so quickly, the Reagans weren't even given time to mourn their loss. As President and First Lady they knew, of course, that you don't have much of a private life, but it seemed especially sad that they could not have any time to themselves to mourn.

Just before the end of his second term, in January 1989, we sent a couple of people who had been selected to be on his postpresidential staff ahead to Los Angeles to set up his new office.

Then, about a week after the rest of us had been home, the President came to the office to start a regular schedule. He had only seen their new home once or twice before they moved in, and he wanted to get acclimated to his new surroundings. The Reagans were going through many things they hadn't seen in eight years, for much of their furniture, books, and memorabilia had been stored when they left for Washington. For a time, each day he would bring in a box or two of things he wanted to set up on the floor-to-ceiling bookshelves in his new office.

During that first year in Los Angeles, much time was spent going through papers and getting used to the new office. He had a number of speaking engagements, mostly day trips to such places as Phoenix, Las Vegas, or Palm Springs.

Before Christmas that year (1989), he walked through the lobby of our building one day and saw the Toys for Tots barrels. He asked me about them. I reminded him that once a year the Commandant of the Marine Corps had come to the Oval Office to receive some gifts from the Reagans for the Toys for Tots drive. In those days, the President hadn't seen the barrel, because the one at the White House was in the West Wing lobby, and he didn't come in that way.

He said, "When I go home today, I'll have to ask Nancy if we have some toys around the house." About an hour after he got home, he called me and said, "We looked everywhere, but there's not a toy in the house. What are we going to do?" "I guess we're going shopping," I replied. And so we did, the next day. As President, he didn't have an opportunity to do such things because of security considerations and the desire not to disrupt other people's lives.

I reminded him of the beautiful shopping center about a block from our office and that there was a Disney store there where we could get stuffed animals. I remembered also that, next to the Disney store, there was a Fifties-style diner where they had great hamburgers. Usually, we had a soup-and-salad lunch brought into the office for him, but I knew he loved hamburgers and suggested we stop for lunch on the way to our shopping. Few people noticed us in the diner at first, but suddenly everyone there seemed to recognize him. As we got ready to leave, people came up to shake his hand and wish him well.

In the Disney store, he said, "What do you think?" I pointed to a bin filled with stuffed animals. I suggested he pick out two that he thought kids would love. Next thing I knew, there he was, standing in line, with Mickey Mouse under one arm and Minnie under the other, waiting to pay for his purchase.

I said that, as long as we were at the shopping center, he might want to go to the See's Candies store to get a box for the White House telephone operators (he had always sent them a big box at Christmas). The See's store was very busy. I suggested we get a ten-pound box, but none were in sight. I saw a woman in a white uniform leaning over a shelf stocking it, and tapped her on the shoulder. "I wonder if you could help this gentleman?" I said. She wasn't happy at being interrupted as she straightened up. She looked at me, then to the man next to me, and her expression went from why-are-you-bugging-me-lady to oh-my-gosh-it's-the-President. She was grinning from ear to ear and couldn't have been more helpful.

As we left, a crowd had begun to gather. The Secret Service always gets a little apprehensive when it is hard to move about in a crowd, but just then we were walking by a chocolate-chip cookie store. Chocolate chips are one of his favorites, so I suggested that, as long as we were there, why not get some cookies to take back to the staff? He liked the idea (it meant he'd get one, too). That was the President's first real outing as a private citizen, and he had a wonderful time (and so did those of us who accompanied him!).

COLIN L. POWELL

GENERAL, U.S. ARMY (RETIRED); CHAIRMAN, JOINT
CHIEFS OF STAFF, DEPARTMENT OF DEFENSE,
1989—93

"Colin, is it still okay for me to salute?"

Born in New York City in 1937, the son of Jamaican immigrants, Colin Powell attended New York public schools and earned his bachelor's degree from the City College of New York in geology. (He later earned a master's degree in business administration at George Washington University.) He was in the ROTC program at CCNY and received his commission as a second lieutenant in 1958. His Army career included two tours of duty in Vietnam and one in Korea. He commanded the 2nd Brigade of the 101st Airborne Division at Fort Campbell, Kentucky, and the Army's V Corps in Germany. He later became Commander in Chief, Forces Command, based at Fort McPherson, Georgia. In 1972, he was a White House fellow. In December 1987, President Reagan appointed him assistant to the President for national security affairs. He was named Chairman of the Joint Chiefs by President George Bush in October 1989.

A few months after President Reagan left the White House and I had returned to the Army, I was in Los Angeles on business and went to visit him. I was met at the airport by a young Army sergeant from the local recruiting office who had been selected to be my driver for the day. For him this was the big time, driving around a four-star general who, until recently, had been the national security adviser to the President and was now commander of all Army field forces in the United States.

As we drove to the Reagan home, the young sergeant and I talked about his job. He told me how he went about encouraging high school students to consider an Army career. He wasn't a professional recruiter, but a paratrooper from the 82nd Airborne Division who was doing a two-year stint in recruiting. He had been selected to drive me as a reward for being a good recruiter.

Nearing the Reagan home, he became quite nervous. He asked for a favor. I said, "Sure, what is it?" He said, "When you see President Reagan, would you please tell him how much we appreciated all he has done for us. He made us feel proud to be in uniform." I said I would do that and that I was sure the President would be very happy to hear it.

The Secret Service cleared us through the gate and we drove up to the door. As we approached, it opened and President Reagan stepped out. We stopped and I got out and walked over to him. The driver was frozen to the wheel of the car. I told President Reagan what the young man had said. I asked him if he would let me call the sergeant over to say hello. "Of course," Reagan said. I motioned to the driver, but it took three waves of my hand to get him to let go of the wheel, get out of the car, and come over to us. As he came up to the President, he stopped, came to attention, and saluted Reagan. The President drew himself up and returned the salute. They exchanged conversation for a few moments and then the sergeant returned to the car.

As Reagan and I entered the house, he relayed the story about how he learned to salute. "You pick it up and you throw it away," he said, while repeating the salute motion. Then he caught himself up and said, "Colin, is it still okay for me to salute?" "Mr. President," I said, "please don't ever stop. It meant a lot to us." He relaxed, and as we walked along he added, "You know, the only advice I gave George [Bush] was that he should continue the saluting." And then he said, shyly, "Is he?" "Yes, Mr. President, he is." Reagan was pleased. "Good. That's good," he said. We then joined Nancy in the living room.

I have told this story before and, when I have, it has never failed to bring a warm glow—and a tear—to any soldiers in the room.

NANCY CLARK REYNOLDS
FORMER AIDE; FRIEND

"If he sees someone in discomfort or misery, he'll stop
and try to remedy it."

*In 1967, Nancy Clark Reynolds left her position as a news anchor and political
reporter at a San Francisco television station to become assistant press secretary to
California's new governor, Ronald Reagan. She later became a special assistant to
the governor, working in his administration through both terms. In 1975, she
became an account executive at Deaver & Hannaford, the public relations firm that
coordinated Ronald Reagan's business and political activities, where she "advanced" many of his events for the next two years. Moving on to public affairs
assignments in Washington, D.C., for two corporations, she later became a partner
in what is now the Wexler Group before retiring in 1992. During the Reagan
administration in Washington, she took on several public service assignments, including membership on the President's Commission on White House Fellowships
and the President's Advisory Committee on Trade Negotiations. She also served
as U.S. representative to the United Nations Commission on the Status of Women.*

Ronald Reagan was such a joy to be around. My ten years working for him in various capacities were crowded with so many incidents of his kindness and thoughtfulness that it's hard to remember them all. Mike Deaver and I were the only ones to accompany the Reagans to the Philippines, Vietnam, and Taiwan when Henry Kissinger was in Beijing. That was back in 1971. Nixon had asked the Reagans to go to Taiwan to tell Chiang Kai-shek everything was going to be fine while, at that same moment, Kissinger was making a deal with the Communists in Beijing. Ronald Reagan was gracious and charming throughout. It's not well known that when they returned from that trip, Ronald and Nancy Reagan telephoned the families of every single serviceman they had met in Vietnam. One of them had wanted the governor to call his wife on their anniversary or her birthday. He went one better: He sent her flowers, then called her.

I remember one summer day back in Sacramento, when a young woman was picketing outside the governor's office, which was a corner office on the main floor of the State Capitol, with big windows overlooking a beautiful park. I was in his office on some matter and Governor Reagan said, "It's about a hundred and one degrees out there and I don't think that poor girl has had a glass of water or anything else. Go out there and bring her into the office and let's find out what is troubling her."

I went out and said to her, "The governor can see you from his office [he was looking out at us], and if you'll come with me, you can meet with him." I brought her in. The security people were horrified. Nevertheless, the governor offered her a seat and some water and said, "What's the problem?" It had to do with her husband being in prison. By then Ed Meese had arrived and they all discussed the matter. I don't recall its resolution, but I do know that that gesture was typical of Ronald Reagan. He didn't do it to impress me or the young woman. If he sees someone in discomfort or misery, he'll stop and try to remedy it.

When he gave me his favorite saddle, it was another instance of his kindheartedness. At the ranch we had in Idaho, there was a wood-burning stove in the little house where the cowboys lived, which adjoined the stable. One day when the cowboys were away, the stovepipe broke in two and the house and stable burned down; three horses were killed.

Although I was terribly upset, I had not planned to mention the fire to the Reagans. But I must have looked very downcast, and one of them asked me, "Why are you so down in the dumps?" I told them. Reagan said, "Nancy, I know how you must feel. I love my horses. How terrible." I thought that was the end of it, but it wasn't. Right after that, we went to New York for some speaking engagements he had. When we flew back to Los Angeles and got off the plane, there was Barney [Willard Barnett, Reagan's driver] at the bottom of the ramp holding Ronald Reagan's favorite Italian jumping saddle. The governor said to me, "I know there is nothing to make up for something you love like that, but I'd like you to have this and use it, and perhaps it will inspire you to get a new horse." I was overwhelmed. He had given this from the heart.

Thinking back to those days in the Governor's Office, I used to give him the mail. One day a man wrote to him who wanted a suit to get married in, and the governor sent him a suit—one of his own! A woman wanted some yarn with which to knit things for her kids and was blaming him for the high price of it. She said she didn't have enough money to buy the yarn. So he had somebody go out and buy a huge box of yarn for her.

He always took the time to carefully go through the mail that came to him. That's why those of us on his staff took care to sort it. He would answer any letter that came to his "in" box. I think this came from his Hollywood days. In those days, fan mail was very important. He saw a parallel in these letters to the governor. Indeed, these were the people who had put him in office.

Another time, he received a letter from a woman in the Palm Springs area. Her son wanted a bicycle for Christmas, but she couldn't afford it. The governor said to me, "Nancy, send this to Frank Sinatra. I'll bet he'll love it and do something about it." He did. Sinatra showed up at the woman's door and presented them with the bicycle and other gifts, all from him. At first, the woman didn't recognize him!

In Washington, I didn't work in the administration, but still saw a good deal of the Reagans. I introduced Tom Clancy, the author, to President Reagan. A friend had given me Tom's book, *The Hunt for Red October,* and I liked it so much I bought copies for my sons, my uncle, and Ronald Reagan. It was Christmastime. When I went over to the White House to have Christmas dinner with the Reagans, the President said, "If I don't look as if I'd had much sleep, it's because I couldn't put that book down. I want to meet Tom Clancy. Can you arrange it?" So I called Tom at his insurance office (writing was then just an avocation for him). We arranged for him to meet for lunch in the Roosevelt Room with the President and several other White House officials who had been reading the book.

Ed Hickey (gubernatorial security chief and later chairman of the Federal Maritime Commission) and I went to see the President after he was shot. Nancy said it was okay. I don't recall how we paired up, but I do remember my surprise at walking into what I thought was the tiniest of hospital rooms, with all the blinds closed. It was very dark and there he was, being pounded on the back by a nurse. During that time they were trying to get him to sit up and cough. It was necessary that he cough every twenty minutes (they were worried about pneumonia). He was in great pain. It showed. He was drawn and pale. At first he didn't realize we were in the room. Then he looked up from his coughing and said, "Well now, there's a sight for sore eyes. If it isn't Boston Blackie and the other Nancy in my life."

The ability to create laughter was one of his great secret weapons. People who didn't agree with him always came away with something such as "I tried to dislike him, but I couldn't." Tip O'Neill, when he was speaker of the House, would say terrible things about Reagan publicly, but then go on to say how much he liked the man.

WILLIAM RUSHER

NATIONAL REVIEW PUBLISHER EMERITUS, COLUMNIST, SCHOLAR

"I haven't changed my mind one damn bit about Taiwan."

From 1957 to 1988, William Rusher was the publisher of William F. Buckley's National Review. *Since 1973, he has been a nationally syndicated newspaper columnist and, since 1989, a distinguished fellow of the Claremont Institute for the Study of Statesmanship and Political Philosophy. A lawyer by training, he has received the New York University School of Law's Distinguished Citizen Award "in recognition of his able articulation of the conservative viewpoint."*

In 1981, just before Ronald Reagan left for Washington for his inauguration as President, the political establishment of California had a farewell dinner in his honor. Jesse Unruh, the formidable Democratic politician who had once run against Reagan for governor, was one of the speakers. In his tribute, he said that any politician can say "no" to his enemies, but that Ronald Reagan had the ability to say "no" to his friends.

That resonated with me because, five years earlier, I had been seized with the conviction that the Republican party was never going to turn conservative. The so-called Rockefeller Republicans, while unable to win a presidential nomination, could arrange to veto anybody who might conceivably turn the country to the right. Therefore, I reasoned, what we needed was a new party: not so much a third party as a replacement for the Republican party. And one that replaced it as fast as the Republicans had replaced the Whigs after 1854.

I wrote a book to that effect, which was implicitly addressed to Reagan. He was the man I thought could bring together a coalition of economic and social conservatives, which I saw as necessary to make this a conservative country. Now we know, in retrospect, that that is precisely what he did from 1980 on.

I remember talking with him—it must have been in 1975—and saying, "Governor, the Republican party is not going to nominate you in 1976." "Now, that remains to be seen," he replied. Later, I felt vindicated when he lost the nomination to Gerald Ford. But I'm sure he felt vindicated when he went on to win it in 1980. That was something I did not think could be done in the Republican party even then.

When I brought out my book and presented it to him, he did not rule out the new party idea immediately. In February 1975, he addressed the annual Conservative Political Action Conference in Washington and posed the question, "Do we need a new party, or do we need a new message in our own party that is spelled out in bold colors and not pale pastels?" He didn't answer the question, thus terrifying *The New York Times*. And he gave me some hope.

Later that year, when he had not yet declared for the Republican nomination, I had already decided that Ford was going to win it and I was not going to put up with that, so I decided to start a third party. In a telephone call to Reagan, I made it clear that he could have that party's nomination if he wanted it. He said, "You know, you and I have disagreed about that." I found myself nodding in agreement. Here he was telling me he was not going to go along with my great project and I didn't feel the least bit angry. It was that gift of his in action, of being able to say no to his friends!

Another episode that particularly sticks in my mind took place early in his first term as President. The second Shanghai Communiqué had come out, more or less defining our relationship with Communist China. To some extent it built on "Shanghai I," which was Nixon's great concession to the Chinese. At about the time this new one came out, I was scheduled to go to Taiwan to attend a journalists' conference. I had written a column favorable to Reagan and it must have pleased him, because when I got to San Francisco on my way to Taiwan, my hotel had a message for me to call Camp David. I did and he came on the line and said, "Bill, what are you doing in San Francisco?" "Well, Mr. President," I said, "I'm on my way to Taiwan for a conference. We're going to discuss the news media." I added that I thought this new communiqué that had just come out was rather worrisome from Taiwan's point of view and I hoped it did not signify a change in our policy. He said, "You can tell your friends there I have not changed my mind one damn bit about Taiwan. Whatever weapons they need to defend themselves against attacks or invasion by Red China, they will get from the United States. That is not modified at all by this second communiqué."

That was important news. I said, "What if the technology changes and they need more in the future than they need now?" "They will get what they need," he replied. He was careful to distinguish between what they might need and what they might want.

In Taiwan, I was met at the airport by a government protocol officer. On the way into Taipei, I mentioned this remark of Reagan's. He apparently passed it up the line because the next thing I knew I was in a private conference room with Jimmy Wei, an adviser to President Chiang Ching-kuo, who listened attentively to my description of the conversation. Then I was asked to repeat it to Premier Sun and other senior officials. They didn't say anything, just listened very closely to what I had to say, and I felt fully authorized to tell them, inasmuch as President Reagan had said, "Tell your friends in Taiwan for me that I have not changed my mind one damn bit about Taiwan."

FRED RYAN
CHIEF OF STAFF, 1989–94

"Berliners were lining the road, giving him a hero's welcome. They saw him as the person who made freedom possible in their country."

A southern Californian, Frederick J. Ryan, Jr., began his association with Ronald Reagan in 1980 when he was with a Los Angeles law firm and volunteered to do "advance" work for Reagan-Bush campaign events. In 1982, he joined the White House staff as an assistant to the President. He directed presidential appointments and scheduling activities, as well as the White House Private Sector Initiatives program. Today, he is vice chairman of Allbritton Communications Company, a television and cable firm based in Washington, D.C.

After working for Ronald Reagan for over fifteen years, I think the most striking thing about him is his genuineness. He is the same in private as he is in public. Some politicians are warm and friendly in public and pound the table in private. That's not

Ronald Reagan. His earnestness and courtesy were always apparent, particularly when it came to keeping people waiting. He didn't want that to happen. I recall one time when he was giving a speech in Arizona to an audience of about two thousand people. As we were heading back to Los Angeles, he kept looking at his watch, asking the Secret Service how soon we'd get there, because there was a Boy Scout scheduled to call on him as soon as he got back to his office. It was the only day the boy and his family would be in town, so as soon as we got to the building, the President raced up the elevator to keep his appointment.

After he left the presidency, he made a memorable trip to Germany and Eastern Europe. It was shortly after the Berlin Wall had come down. When we got there, he went up to the Wall with a hammer, just like all those Berliners who were chipping and chiseling away at it. He began pounding at the Wall. This was before the unification of Germany, but by then people could go back and forth freely. When the East German guards caught sight of Ronald Reagan, they jumped down from the Wall and rushed over to shake his hand.

Shortly after that, he walked through the Brandenburg Gate (it was only about three years before that he had stood before the gate and said, "Mr. Gorbachev, open this gate; Mr. Gorbachev, tear down this wall!"). He met in East Berlin with the German Senate. Berliners were lining the road, waving, and giving him a hero's welcome. They saw him as the person who made freedom possible in their country. It was quite a sight.

He went on to Poland, including a visit to the Gdansk shipyard. There were ten thousand people waiting for him in a downpour. Lech Walesa said to him, "Why don't we talk first and then go out for the rally," but President Reagan kept looking out the window at all the people waiting for him in the rain. He decided they should go out right away and did. Just then, the sun broke through and the skies cleared. He got another tumultuous reception.

From there we went to Moscow where he called on Gorbachev, who was still in office, and where the Communists were still running the government. As he walked down the Arbat, people lined the street and hung out of windows—thousands of them—and many waving homemade American flags. Here, too, he was the people's hero.

Not long after he had left the White House and opened his new office in Los Angeles, President Reagan began receiving a stream of dignitaries from Central and Eastern Europe: Václav Havel from Czech Republic, Lech Walesa from Poland, Bulgarian leaders and others. Gorbachev came to visit him, too. President Reagan took Gorbachev up to the ranch and gave him a cowboy hat.

For several years, he had a busy speaking schedule. By 1992, he figured that his appearance at the Republican National Convention might be his last and he gave a very stirring speech. In a way it was a summing up of his political life.

Another thing about his active retirement years: He set a policy soon after arriving back in California that if anybody who had ever worked for him wanted to call on him, he would be available. So a lot of people who had worked in various departments or agencies for years but had never personally met him came to call on him at his office in Los Angeles.

A funny thing happened when that office opened. At first the phones weren't working quite right. For the first few days, many calls were ringing directly into his office. He would answer when it rang. One fellow said he wanted to speak to Ronald Reagan and the President said it was he. At first the man couldn't believe it, but then said he wanted to come see him. "All right, when would you like to come in," the President said. "Tomorrow," the man said. "That's fine," was the reply, and the man came in the next day. He said he just wanted to tell Ronald Reagan face-to-face what a great President he'd been. About then the phones were fixed. The next day, the same man called again and said he'd like to come in again. This time the secretary said, "Well, lightning struck once when you got the President, but I'm afraid it didn't strike a second time."

The last year or so before he wrote his letter saying he had Alzheimer's disease, he did a number of truly memorable things. There was the speech to the Republican convention in Houston in 1992. Then he opened the Republican gala in Washington in early 1994 with a beautiful valedictory speech, and he gave his last speech on world affairs at the Citadel. The speech was deeply moving. It, too, was a farewell. The cadets were up on their feet saluting him.

Reagan always rose to the occasion. It was certainly true with the letter to the American people about his Alzheimer's affliction, instead of trying to conceal the condition, which he could have done. After all, he had Secret Service to protect his privacy if he wanted. And he could have said he was retiring and just wanted to go to his ranch and ride horses. That wasn't his way. He was up front; he wrote the letter and made it public. His decision was the right one, and the public outpouring of support certainly verified it.

ELAINE CRISPEN SAWYER
PRESS SECRETARY TO THE FIRST LADY, 1985—89

"He knew his beloved Nancy was going to be all
right, so he wasn't going to allow his personal worries
to make anyone else uneasy."

*Elaine Sawyer first worked for the Reagans at the Los Angeles–based public re-
lations firm of Deaver & Hannaford in 1976. She joined the 1980 Reagan
presidential campaign as special assistant to the Reagans, then, in January 1981,
accompanied them on the Inaugural flight to Washington to begin working in the
White House in the new administration.*

Over the years, I accompanied the Reagans on many trips
within our borders and throughout the world. One set of trips
that stands out as especially vivid and poignant involved the President's daily visits to Mrs. Reagan at Bethesda Naval Hospital,
while she was recovering from breast cancer surgery. I would
spend the day with her and he would come out after office hours

on *Marine One,* the Presidential helicopter. He would have dinner with her; then the President would head back to the White House on *Marine One,* and I would ride back with him.

On one of those first return trips, I headed for a seat toward the back, but the staff urged me to go up front, sit in Mrs. Reagan's seat and cheer him up. I couldn't think of anything to say, so I commented on all the twinkling lights below. He gently corrected me, pointing out that the lights weren't really twinkling, that the effect was caused by the atmosphere. He went on to explain how they would appear different from summer to winter, when the leaves were off the trees. Here he was, with plenty on his mind, cheering up the rest of us. I thought at the time that he knew that his beloved Nancy was going to be all right, so he wasn't going to allow his personal worries to make anyone else uneasy.

That was so typical of him, putting people at ease, from world leaders to youngsters. One year, the Reagans invited my daughter Cheryl and me to their ranch for Thanksgiving dinner. Although Cheryl had met the Reagans many times at receptions and other events, she was excited and a bit apprehensive. "Mom, we'll be there for four or five hours. What am I going to talk with the President about for that long?" she said. I told her she needn't worry about it, and it turned out that it was like being with a favorite uncle.

The President took us on a tour of the tack room; he showed us his saddles, and his famous woodpile where he did so much chopping. At the table, he said grace and carved the turkey, then regaled us with stories about Hollywood days, summits with Gorbachev, even world economics. Cheryl was so enchanted that, to this day, she can't remember if she said much of anything at all!

President Reagan's sense of humor was never far below the surface. I recall an incident during the 1987 Washington summit with Gorbachev. While the two leaders were to meet in the morning, Mrs. Reagan had invited Raisa Gorbachev to join her for coffee (White House protocol called for coffee to be served in the morning, tea in the afternoon). When the Gorbachevs arrived at the diplomatic entrance to the White House, the ladies went upstairs for their visit. At the conclusion of the men's meeting, I was in the diplomatic reception room with them, waiting for the ladies. President Reagan looked at his watch and asked me to let Mrs. Reagan know it was time for President Gorbachev to leave for his next meeting. I went straight upstairs to find the ladies deep in conversation. I caught Mrs. Reagan's eye, then went downstairs to say that the ladies needed just a few more minutes. About ten minutes passed. President Reagan looked at his watch again and reminded me—a bit more sternly—that we were keeping his guest from his next appointment. I dashed up the stairs again, but was waved off by the ladies. I went back downstairs to say they would be down "shortly." Five minutes later, the President said, "Elaine . . ." I knew this was my last chance, so I ran up the stairs one more time and implored the ladies to join their husbands. As they walked into the diplomatic reception room, there were Presidents Reagan and Gorbachev, their suit sleeves pushed back and each tapping his wristwatch! They tried to look stern, but the smiles broke through and everyone had a hearty laugh.

RICHARD SCHWEIKER
CABINET SECRETARY, U.S. SENATOR,
VICE PRESIDENTIAL CANDIDATE

"Dick, we came to Kansas City together and we'll leave together."

In July 1976, as the Republican National Convention in Kansas City, Missouri, neared, Ronald Reagan, locked in a tight race with President Gerald Ford for the party's presidential nomination, took the unprecedented step of naming in advance his vice presidential choice: Senator Richard Schweiker. Nearly five years later, President Ronald Reagan named Dick Schweiker as his first secretary of health and human services. Schweiker served until February 1983, when he resigned to take a position as president of the American Council of Life Insurance. He retired in December 1994. Prior to his Cabinet appointment, he served in the U.S. Congress for twenty years, first in the House of Representatives, 1961–69 (from Pennsylvania's Thirteenth Congressional District), then in the Senate, 1969–81. Before his public service, he had headed a tile-manufacturing company in Pennsylvania. He is a veteran of World War II. He and his wife, Claire, have five children.

One of the things that always impressed me about Ronald Reagan was the great sensitivity he showed toward people with whom he dealt. I think back to July 1976 and the Republican convention in Kansas City. The way he handled my situation, as his chosen running mate, will always stand out in my memory. Our campaign had proposed a change in the convention rules (Rule 15C) to require that President Ford also announce his vice presidential choice in advance. The vote on the floor became a test for the nomination vote the next night. We lost it closely. The next morning, we had a breakfast strategy session. Before anything was discussed, I volunteered to withdraw from the ticket. Without batting an eye, Ronald Reagan said, "Dick, we came to Kansas City together and we'll leave together." That reply was not rehearsed. It was spontaneous and made a great impression on me.

Earlier in July, I had flown to Los Angeles to spend a day with him at his home in Pacific Palisades, at his invitation, to explore the vice presidency matter with him. I was somewhat tense, for, on the surface, we seemed an unlikely match, but he made me feel very much at home and took the tension out of the whole situation. I came away wholeheartedly in support of his plan.

One evening at the convention, while Claire and I were out calling on delegations, the Reagans invited our kids up to their box. The whole Reagan family went out of their way to make the kids feel at home.

When the convention was over and we were all preparing to leave, we first had a gathering of the campaign workers in the hotel ballroom. There was hardly a dry eye in the house. Claire went over to Governor Reagan and thanked him for all he had done and how he had conducted himself. He said, "Well, Claire, you shouldn't be upset about the outcome because it wasn't part of God's plan."

There were so many acts of kindness on his part. For instance, at the 1976 convention, the Reagans and we were to address the

Hawaii delegation. I told the delegates that Claire and I had honeymooned in Hawaii and had named our daughter Lani. As we were leaving, Governor Reagan lifted from his neck the lei the Hawaii delegates had given him and placed it around Lani's neck.

When it came to government business, he was plenty businesslike. I recall in the early 1980s, when I was secretary of health and human services, we were having a Cabinet meeting to discuss reforms in the Medicare program. We were having an in-depth discussion, when his staff decided it was time to bring it to an end. President Reagan would have none of it. He wanted to hear the different opinions and waved off his staff. I saw this happen a number of times. He wanted to be familiar with an issue, not in all its details, but with enough information so he could assess how it would play out. Just when we would get into the heart of a discussion, one of his aides would try to stop it. He didn't like that.

The evening in March 1981, after Reagan was shot, Claire and I were supposed to be with the Reagans for dinner in the family quarters of the White House, along with other Cabinet members and spouses. That was canceled of course, but it wasn't long before he was back at work. What impressed me was that when he walked into the Cabinet Room that first time back, he was exactly like he was before the assassination attempt. I said to myself, "Is this really the man who was shot?" He was just great in his recovery and the command he demonstrated.

GEORGE SHULTZ

SECRETARY OF STATE, 1982—88

"He preferred to get something done than to get credit for it."

George Shultz held two key positions in the Reagan administration: first, as chairman of the President's Economic Policy Advisory Board (1981–82), then as secretary of state (1982–88). In the latter position, he played a major role in implementing the foreign policy that led to the successful conclusion of the cold war and the development of U.S. relationships with the countries of the Asia-Pacific region, especially Japan, China, and the Association of South East Asian Nations (ASEAN).

In addition to his government service (he was also secretary of labor, 1969, director of the Office of Management and Budget, 1970–72, and secretary of the treasury, 1972–74), Mr. Shultz has had distinguished careers in academia and business. He has been dean of the University of Chicago's Graduate School of Business, is a professor of international economics at Stanford University's Graduate School of Business, and is a distinguished fellow of the Hoover Institution. From 1974 to 1982 he was president of the Bechtel Group, the international engineering firm, which he rejoined after his government service. Today, he divides his time between his academic and business careers. In 1989, he received the nation's highest civilian honor, the Medal of Freedom. He is the author of eight books.

My first extended conversation with Ronald Reagan took place in 1974 when I returned to California after serving in the Nixon administration. Nixon was still President when I left Washington. Back home in California, I received a call from Governor Reagan asking me to come to Sacramento to have lunch with him. I did, and I think Ed Meese was the only other person there.

I got the most extensive grilling imaginable about the federal government and how it operates. How does the budget get put together? How does the Cabinet function? What makes for good results and what doesn't? The questions were good ones. It was clear he had a keen interest in the way the government works, especially financing.

Afterward, I said to a friend, "Everybody knows that he wants to be President, and I can see he has a reason, a purpose. He's interested in how you work the presidency, not just in getting elected." It was a very reassuring thing. He was thinking far ahead. He was thinking operationally about how to make the federal government work well.

Thinking back over the years when I was President Reagan's secretary of state, I found he had a firm view on how he wanted to approach the Soviet Union. It suited me. He wanted the United States to be strong in every way. He felt that in dealing with the Soviets (and also the Chinese), negotiating from strength was the only way to do it. He managed to get the United States into a much stronger position than it had been. Once there, he wanted to negotiate with them. I think a lot of his supporters really didn't want to do this. They wanted the strength, but they didn't want to use it in negotiation because that meant give and take. They didn't want to give, but he wasn't afraid of negotiation because he felt he could do it well.

The first indication I got of this was on a snowy night in

Washington. I had just returned from my first visit to China as secretary of state in February 1983. There was quite a lot of television coverage of the visit. The President and I talked over a different way of thinking about our relationship with China. He asked me to lay it out and I did. He adopted it and it proved workable.

The snowstorm had been so bad the Reagans couldn't go to Camp David that weekend, not even by car. They were stuck in the White House. They called us at home and asked my wife, Obie, and me if we could have supper with them that Sunday evening. There were just the four of us. They were full of questions about China and the Soviet Union (as secretary of the treasury for Nixon, I had had quite a few dealings with the Soviets). I said to President Reagan, "You know this dialogue I had with [Soviet Ambassador] Dobrynin which you authorized? He's coming to my office next Tuesday afternoon. How would you like it if I just wheeled him over here and you talk to him?" He said he'd like to do that and added, "I have only one message to give him and that is to tell his boss, Andropov, that I'm ready to have substantive discussions. That's my message."

When Dobrynin came to my office at four o'clock the next Tuesday, I said, "Anatoly, if you are interested we can go down in the basement, get in the car, and go over to see the President." He was a very alert diplomat and this was a big opportunity, so off we went.

Meanwhile, there had been a battle raging in the White House about whether to do this or not. Most of the staff didn't want him to. Bill Clark, then his national security adviser, recommended the President not see Dobrynin. But, contrary to the image that he was just steered around by people, Reagan knew what he wanted to do, and that was that. Dobrynin's meeting, instead of being ten minutes, lasted an hour or so. The discussion ranged over a spectrum of subjects. I didn't say much. The President carried the ball. He did well and he put a lot of emphasis on human rights. At the time there was a group of Pentecostal Russians holed up in our embassy in Moscow. They had gone in during the Carter administration. They couldn't leave without being arrested by the Soviets. He talked about that quite a bit and wanted it solved. He was willing to do it without fanfare.

Afterward, Dobrynin and I worked back and forth on the matter. He called it "our special project." I kept the President informed, of course. He said that, on matters such as this one, the main thing was to get things straightened out, in which case he wouldn't make anything of it. And, after about three months, we got them out. They emigrated to the United States, about fifty families in all. I always saw this deal as, "You let them out, and we won't crow about it." That's the way it worked. Reagan never said a word about it. It had been done very quietly. It just seemed to happen.

This was a good demonstration for the Soviets. It showed them he meant what he said and that his word was good. This was the first deal made between Reagan and the Soviets. It established his bona fides with them and it let them see that he considered human rights important, and why. And human rights always stood high on his agenda. Also high on his agenda was: No grandstanding. He preferred to get something done than to get credit for it. That's the way he always behaved.

JEAN SMITH
REAGAN FAMILY FRIEND

"The secret of his success was his consistent reliance
on his philosophy."

*Jean Smith and her husband, the late William French Smith, who served as
President Reagan's attorney general in his first term, became friends of the Reagans
in the 1960s.*

Although I did not know Ronald Reagan back in the 1950s,
I heard him speak and was very impresssed. The first time, as I
recall, was at a conference of Junior Leagues in Coronado, near
San Diego. They always liked to get colorful personalities as their
keynote speakers. I went expecting to hear nothing but light
patter from an actor. Instead, he mesmerized that audience with
real substance on issues of the day. His philosophy of bringing
government back closer to the people and away from centralized
control in Washington was clear even then.

In the early 1960s, we met the Reagans socially through mutual friends. The friendship deepened, and after Ronald Reagan was elected governor of California in 1966, Bill became his personal attorney. Though we didn't see the Reagans constantly, we always enjoyed their company very much.

I recall one incident that occurred after he became President in which his great sense of humor came into play. It was at a ceremony on the White House grounds. It was a beautiful day, with clear sky and a snapping breeze. There were many children there, all the flags were flying, and the Marine Band was playing. It made you tingle with pride at being an American. This set the stage for the President to speak, but when he came to the podium, he said, "I've just had a lesson on how to become an anticlimax!"

He used that humor very effectively, of course, in politics. He could get his audience laughing over government excesses, or he would skewer an opponent's position on a particular issue with humor, but he never engaged in personal attacks. It would have been completely out of character for him.

He is a tremendously appealing person. The secret of his success, I think, was his consistent reliance on his philosophy. He never wavered from it.

EDWARD TELLER
DIRECTOR EMERITUS, LAWRENCE LIVERMORE
NATIONAL LABORATORY

"I think that was the time he started to think about defense against missiles."

Dr. Edward Teller is best known for his work on the development of nuclear explosives and of a strong defense for America. As a noted physicist, he has more than one hundred technical publications, books, patents and general media articles to his credit. Born in Budapest, he left Europe as the Nazi menace grew. That menace, coupled with the possibilities inherent in fission, led him to work on the Manhattan Project. Subsequently, the possibility of releasing nuclear fusion occupied much of his attention. After World War II, he joined the faculty of the University of Chicago, then moved to the University of California (Berkeley) as one of the founders of the Lawrence Livermore National Laboratory in 1954. Subsequently, he served as its director for two years. In 1982, he was appointed to the White House Science Council and is presently on the National Space Council. He is also a senior research fellow at the Hoover Institution at Stanford University.

It was shortly after he became governor of California in 1967 that I first met Ronald Reagan. I went to Sacramento to invite him to visit the Lawrence Livermore National Laboratory. He came a few months later. We briefed him about our work on stopping a missile attack on the United States. It was a rather long presentation and I remember clearly that he listened quite attentively. Over the course of perhaps two hours, he asked many questions. His questions made it clear the topic was a new one to him. He was interested and understood the point we were driving at, but made no comment as to whether he agreed with it. Nevertheless, I think that was about the time he started to think about defense against missiles. Several of us had lunch with him that day, and everybody liked him.

Then, in March 1983, as President, he announced the Strategic Defense Initiative, a program intended to defend the nation against missile attack. I was there when he made the announcement. Over the years, he had asked others about the subject. For a man who has been accused of being ready to "shoot from the hip," he certainly took his time to make up his mind about this—fifteen and a half years to be exact! But, in 1983, his ideas were clear and his actions decisive.

He agreed with our original idea at Livermore that the United States must have such a defense and he was confident we could achieve it, but he also felt we were trying to stop incoming missiles with nuclear explosions. He did not say to us, don't do it that way, but he did say that, if possible, do it without nuclear explosions. It was clear he wanted it done another way. That had an effect on us.

We have since proven that the job can be done with a direct hit, without using a nuclear explosion. Our scientists have developed what is called "brilliant pebbles." "Pebbles" because they are small, "brilliant" because they have to be more than clever to hit the incoming missile. That was our response to his response to our original plan.

Toward the end of his second term, he asked a few of us to come to the White House to receive the Presidential Citizens

Medal. Instead of reading citations with the medals, he said, "This is my 2,835th day in office and on this occasion, I'll tell you a story about a cantankerous old woman who went to a judge.

" 'Your Honor, I want a divorce,' she said.

" 'How old are you, madam?'

" 'Ninety years.'

" 'How old is your husband?'

" 'Ninety-two.'

" 'How long have you been married?'

" 'Seventy-three years.'

" 'Any children?'

" 'Oh, yes, Your Honor. Six children and they are all right. Twenty-six grandchildren; five great-grandchildren and one more coming.'

" 'Madam, do I understand you want to be divorced?'

" 'Yes, Your Honor. Enough is enough.' "

Upon telling the story, he distributed the medals without further comment.

After quite a bit of thought, I came to the conclusion that what Ronald Reagan meant was this: Enough *is* enough. Be satisfied and don't worry if you are not asked to do anything more. His humor always had a definite purpose.

MARGARET THATCHER
PRIME MINISTER OF BRITAIN, 1979–90

"Ronald Reagan . . . demonstrated just how potent a weapon in international politics human rights could be."

Today a member of the House of Lords, Lady Thatcher—The Right Honorable The Baroness Thatcher, L.G., O.M., P.C., F.R.S.—became Britain's first woman prime minister when her Conservative party won the parliamentary elections of May 1979. She subsequently carried her party to successive victories in general elections in 1983 and 1987. She resigned in November 1990 and was elevated to the House of Lords in 1992. She and Ronald Reagan first met in her offices in the House of Commons in 1975 when her party was still in opposition. They had immediate rapport, a rapport that deepened into one of the most remarkably effective international political friendships of modern times.

I . . . met Governor Reagan shortly after my becoming Conservative leader in 1975. Even before then, I knew something about him because Denis [Thatcher] had returned home one evening in the late 1960s full of praise for a remarkable speech Ronald Reagan had just delivered at the Institute of Directors. I read the text myself and quickly saw what Denis meant. When we met in person I was immediately won over by his charm, sense of humour and directness. In the succeeding years I read his speeches, advocating tax cuts as the root to wealth creation and stronger defenses as an alternative to *detente*. I also read many of his . . . [radio] broadcasts . . . which his Press Secretary sent over regularly for me. I agreed with them all. In November 1978 we met again in my room in the House of Commons.

In the early years Ronald Reagan had been dismissed by much of the American political elite, though not by the American electorate, as a right-wing maverick who could not be taken seriously. Now he was seen by many thoughtful Republicans as their best ticket back to the White House. Whatever Ronald Reagan had gained in experience, he had not done so at the expense of his beliefs. I found them stronger than ever. When he left my study, I reflected on how different things might look if such a man were President of the United States. But, in November 1978, such a prospect seemed a long way off.

The so-called Reagan Doctrine, which Ronald Reagan developed in a speech to both Houses of Parliament in 1982, demonstrated just how potent a weapon in international politics human rights could be. His view was that we should fight the battle of ideas for freedom against communism throughout the world, and refuse to accept the permanent exclusion of the captive nations from the benefits of freedom.

This unashamedly philosophical approach and the armed strength supporting it transformed the political world. President Reagan undermined the Soviet Union at home by giving hope to its citizens, directly assisted rebellions against illegitimate Communist regimes in Afghanistan and Nicaragua, and facilitated the peaceful transition to democracy in Latin American countries and the Philippines. Of course, previous American governments had extolled human rights, and President Carter had even declared that they were the "soul" of U.S. foreign policy. Where President Reagan went beyond these, however, was in making the Soviets the principal target of his human rights campaign, and in moving from rhetorical to material support for anti-Communist guerrillas in countries where Communist regimes had not securely established themselves. The result was a decisive advance for freedom in the world. . . . In this instance, human rights and wider American purposes were in complete harmony.

[Reprinted from *The Path to Power* (New York: HarperCollins, 1995, pp. 372, 527–528) with the kind permission of The Right Honorable The Baroness Thatcher.]

W. F. ROLLINS

R. EMMETT TYRRELL, JR.
WRITER, EDITOR

"He was in command."

Bob Tyrrell is founder and editor in chief of The American Spectator, *a political and cultural monthly magazine. He is also a syndicated columnist, a frequent guest on television public affairs programs, and the author of several books, including* Boy Clinton, The Conservative Crack-up, The Liberal Crack-up, *and* Public Nuisances.

I first met Ronald Reagan in 1968. Some of us had set up a Reagan for President Committee (we were college students, at Indiana University). As I recall, he came through Indianapolis and had a lunch or dinner for young people who were supporting him. Many people today don't remember or realize that he let his supporters put him up for the Republican nomination that year, even though, at the time, he had been governor of California for less than two years. This was just after some friends and

I had founded *The Alternative* (which today is *The American Spectator*). It was a counter-counterculture magazine. As I look back on that event, I see a luminous figure there. He gave us a sense that great things could be accomplished.

He seems to have been touched by a certain kind of genius, like Franklin Roosevelt. The comparisons between the two of them are as many as are the differences in their policies. Both men were criticized for being facile. Both were criticized for being disorganized and having bad staffing. The liberals called the disorganization of the FDR administration "creative." When it showed up in Reagan's administration (as with the Iran-Contra issue), it was seen as just disorganization. The truth is that both Reagan and Roosevelt brought people of different abilities, points of view, and strategies into a room, heard them all out, then made up their own minds.

Reagan had, as FDR had, that wonderful ability to communicate. Both men also had the ability to write and were pretty good editors, too. But the greatest thing they had in common was a great sense of timing. They knew just when to move. In Reagan's case, take the timing of the Grenada invasion or the timing involved in his holding out for his economic program against heavy odds and with some around him pressing him to cave in.

The critics can complain all they want about his "disorganization" or whatever nonsense they want to pick on, but the fact is he chose the things he wanted to do, had the discipline to stick to a short list, and accomplished what he set out to do: rebuilding our armed forces, beating down inflation, creating long-running economic growth, and, in effect, winning the cold war.

Early in his administration some of the conservative intellectuals were restless because they thought he was moving leftward in some of his policies. I wrote a column about that one day and he called me. He asked me what he should do. I said I thought he'd find it worthwhile to have a regular meeting with a brain trust of writers and editors on his political side of the fence. He asked me to put it together. I'll never forget that first meeting. It was in the Cabinet Room. The day it was to take place I got fevered calls from various Washington operators such as Dick Darman who said, "Oh, do stop by and see me while you're at the White House. I'm an intellectual, too." He didn't attend the meeting, but the "troika" of Baker, Deaver, and Meese did. So did Martin Anderson (then domestic policy adviser) and David Stockman (then heading the Office of Management and Budget). I brought Midge Decter, Irving Kristol, William Rusher, and Frank Shakespeare. The President told me I was in charge and put me in the Vice President's chair.

He took obvious delight in the give-and-take of ideas. Some of his staff people were squirming, but he relished the exchange of ideas with his guests. At the end, he said, "We've got to do this again," and told his staff to arrange it. Afterward, there were a lot of machinations by members of the staff who thought such meetings were a waste of time. We did meet one more time, in the Roosevelt Room but, as I recall, President Reagan did not attend.

The short shrift some of these people gave the idea of regular sessions with conservative intellectuals is symptomatic of a Republican party problem: They have never known how to work with a small cadre of intellectuals who could help them have an effect on the culture of the country. And it is the leftward tilt of the culture that ends up causing the Republicans so many policy problems.

Ever since I've known him, Ronald Reagan liked to read about ideas. He kept up with many periodicals. He read a lot, although I don't know if he had time in the later White House years. During those later years, there were fewer people around him who understood him. Frankly, there were fewer and fewer Californians.

I recall being invited to have coffee with him after the Iran-Contra story broke. I was stunned that his aides—who seemed to have no understanding of him—had convinced him he had to sit there and spew out all manner of facts about government. He had the facts down, all right, but he looked tired and it just wasn't him. It wasn't the sunny, can-do, commanding Ronald Reagan I was used to. I said to myself that he'd no doubt bounce back—

and he did—but on this occasion his staff had overreacted and overprepared him on everything.

One stormy night, he came to dinner at my house. Mrs. Reagan was in New York and he came alone (that is, with only the security entourage, which was no small group). They were everywhere, along with cars, motorcycles, helicopters. For security reasons, they brought him in through the garage. He looked at me and said, with great sincerity, "Bob, I'm terribly sorry about all this." It was a wonderful, relaxed evening, just the same, and he was such a great conversationalist that everyone at the table was involved.

After he retired from the White House, I went to California to visit him and he was his cheerful self. Recalling that after the attempt on his life in 1981 he had begun lifting weights and doing bench presses, I said that his official biographer, Edmund Morris, had told me that Reagan had put an inch and a half on his chest. "Nope, it's two inches," he replied. And he looked it.

He was such good company. I'd hop on a plane tomorrow to be with him. There is no question that Ronald Reagan was one of the great political minds of our century. He was in command.

MIKE WALLACE

SENIOR CORRESPONDENT, CBS TELEVISION'S
60 MINUTES

"History will . . . be kinder to Ronald Reagan than
the recognition he got as President."

Mike Wallace has been coeditor of 60 Minutes *since its premiere in 1968.
His career in journalism began in Chicago in the 1940s as a radio newswriter
and broadcaster for the* Chicago Sun. *He served as a naval communications
officer in World War II, then became a news reporter for radio station
WMAQ, Chicago. He headed several CBS televison programs and reported
from Vietnam in the 1960s before* 60 Minutes *had its first broadcast in September 1968. He has received numerous awards for his reporting, including
eighteen Emmy awards.*

It was a long time ago that I first met Ronald Reagan. It was
in Florida, where I was to be the master of ceremonies for a film
he had starred in. He and several others connected with the

movie were on the stage and I introduced them all. I didn't see him again for some time; not until Edie Davis, Nancy's mother, got us together. Edie was a dear friend of mine.

In Chicago, back in the 1940s, when I was trying to find my niche in broadcasting, I encountered an actress, Edith Davis, who was starring in a radio network soap opera that originated from WBBM. Edie was a warm, gregarious woman, and although she was old enough to be my mother (I'd just turned twenty-four), we became close friends. Through Edie, I came to know her husband, a conservative and proper neurosurgeon, Dr. Loyal Davis, an extraordinary man who ran the Northwestern University Medical School's "brain department," so to speak, and I also met their daughter, Nancy, who was then a student at Smith College.

Time passed, I moved to New York, Loyal and Edie retired to Scottsdale, and Nancy went to Hollywood to try her luck with the movies. The next thing I heard, she was getting married to actor Ronald Reagan.

As time went by, Reagan's acting career began to languish. Then came the 1960s and his initial foray into politics. Since I was covering some political stories for CBS News, our paths began to cross. Of course, the fact that I was an old friend of Nancy and her family gave me an advantage, and I began to build a reporter/source contact with the Reagan camp through his years as governor of California.

After Governor Reagan lost the nomination fight in Kansas City in 1976, Nancy called to ask if I might arrange a dinner for them with some media people in New York City. When I began to phone around, almost no one was particularly interested. I told them they were wrong; that this guy was smart as could be and was going to be a political force to reckon with. Finally, Fred Friendly and his wife and Bill and Judith Moyers came to dinner with Ronnie, Nancy, Lorraine, and me. I've seldom seen a man charm the skeptics as he did. There were just eight of us around the dining table; it was lively, political, and civilized, and Moyers wound up doing an hour show on Reagan as a result. Fred Friendly didn't change his political views, but he liked Reagan, the man, just the same.

Looking back . . . I used to cover the annual governors con-ferences, and one time it was held at the Century Plaza Hotel in Los Angeles. I was there for CBS News with the East Coast-based reportorial crowd, most of them very skeptical about Rea-gan, who was the host governor. On the opening day, he held a news conference and you could see the skeptics beginning to change their minds. Fact is, seldom have I seen a politician so underestimated by the press.

Between his time as governor of California and President (in 1975 as I recall), I did a piece on *60 Minutes* on the Reagans, at their ranch near Santa Barbara, where I talked to them about their days in Hollywood and their life together since, and I asked, "Tell me the last time we had a leader in whom we had a good deal of faith." His reply: "Franklin Delano Roosevelt took his case to the people. When the New Deal started, he was faced with a Congress that wouldn't go along. He went over their heads with his fireside chats. They were the most popular pro-grams on radio. He took his case to the people, he enlightened them, and they made Congress feel the heat. It isn't necessary to enlighten Congress, just put the heat on. Roosevelt got the things he wanted."

Those words came back to me five years later when he made a point of mentioning FDR in his acceptance speech for the Republican presidential nomination in Detroit. And then, during his first months in office, he did precisely what Roosevelt had done; he went over the heads of Congress to get popular support for his programs.

In his 1976 effort for the nomination, he had demonstrated that he had the stamina and drive to carry on a long, arduous campaign, and he kept the pressure on right up to the convention in Kansas City. I interviewed him again a month after the 1976 election, when Carter had beaten Ford. He said he thought that if he had been the nominee he would have beaten Carter. How would he have done it? He said he would have broken into the Solid South (which Carter won), in such states as Texas and Mis-sissippi. "But," he said, "I believe the main point is that Water-gate would not have been an issue had I been the candidate."

"You're thinking of Ford's pardon of Nixon?" I asked. "Yes. I don't say this with any criticism of Gerald Ford, but we could have deprived the Democrats of that issue."

I interviewed him once again at his home in Pacific Palisades, two days before they left for the Republican convention in Detroit in 1980. The anti-Carter mood was strong in the country and many people felt Reagan would go on to win, and I knew that many were alarmed at this prospect. In preparing for the interview, I felt I had to reflect some of that concern. I told myself that it was no time to go easy on Reagan or his wife, my old friend from Chicago. I think reporters sometimes lean over backward to be a bit harder on their friends and, indeed, when I interviewed Nancy separately that day, I ungallantly resorted to sarcasm. We were discussing the awesome responsibility of the presidency, and I pointed out that when we look back over the history of the office, we talk about George Washington, Abraham Lincoln, Franklin Roosevelt . . . "and *Ronald Reagan?*" "Yes," she replied, with a vigorous nod. Far from striking her as incongruous, she found the juxtaposition both natural and appropriate.

I put the question to Reagan himself, but phrased it differently. Instead of citing history, I stressed the contemporary burdens of the presidency. I asked, "Isn't there a certain arrogance in a man whose total formal government experience is eight years in Sacramento as governor of California wanting to take over the direction of foreign and domestic policy of the greatest superpower in the world?" "Well," he replied, "I don't think it's arrogance, and I find myself very conscious of the size and difficulty of the undertaking." "But what about your limitations?" I asked. "Yes, but bear in mind I'm not politically ambitious," he said. "What— not politically ambitious?" I asked in astonishment. "You want to be President of the United States." "That's right, but I'm not on any ego trip or glory ride. I'm running because I think there is a job to do and I want to do it," he said.

We moved along. "Can you explain, Governor, why this competent, decent, mainly successful, two-time governor of California—a man acknowledged by the reporters who have covered him through the years to be bright, serious, and dead honest—

why should that man still have the reputation among millions of Americans as a 'Neanderthal' or even a dangerous hip-shooter, lightweight actor—in short, probably not up to the job of President of the United States?" I thought that was a reasonable question. "Mike, I find the farther away I get from California the more that image exists. Now, maybe now, it's starting to change," he replied. Despite the tough questions, there never was the slightest bit of antagonism on his part. In fact, after the interview, we all went out to dinner at Chasen's. He never held a grudge.

I wound up with great respect for the job Ronald Reagan did as President. It's quite apparent today, as you look around, that we need the kind of man he is. When we talked in 1996 about Colin Powell, we recognized some of that quality in him: a man comfortable with who he is. History, I think, will be kinder to Ronald Reagan than the recognition he got while he was President. A *great* President? Perhaps not; but surely better than most.

CASPAR W. WEINBERGER
CHAIRMAN, *FORBES* MAGAZINE; U.S. SECRETARY
OF DEFENSE (1981–87)

"I didn't come here to get reelected."

"Cap" Weinberger served as secretary of defense throughout nearly all of Ronald Reagan's two terms as President. He began public service with election to the California Assembly in 1952. He served three terms. Governor Reagan appointed him as director of finance of California in 1968. He served until early 1970 when he was appointed by President Nixon as chairman of the Federal Trade Commission. He moved from there to the Office of Management and Budget, first as deputy director, then as director. President Nixon appointed him secretary of health, education, and welfare in 1973. He continued to head the department under President Ford, until leaving to enter private business in August 1975. He then served as vice president and general counsel and a director of the Bechtel Group until joining the Reagan Cabinet in January 1981. He joined Forbes *as its publisher in 1989 and became chairman in 1993.*

I first got to know Ronald Reagan in the early 1960s when I was vice chairman and then state chairman of the California Republican party and he was getting active on behalf of our candidates. He went out and talked with various county committees and volunteer groups. He would go anywhere, do anything we asked him, including covering the smallest mountain counties. He didn't like to fly in those days, so he had plenty of long auto trips. When he arrived, there were always big crowds that came out to hear him. As soon as he entered the room, you could almost feel the aura about him. He could transform a rather stiff group into enthusiasts with that great smile and engaging manner of his.

Some recollections from his years as governor come to mind. Early in his first term, the legislature was seriously considering—in response to pressure from the teachers' union—an increase in teacher salaries. There had also been a lot of talk about the schools not being very effective. We were still feeling the aftereffects of sputnik (the Soviet satellite, launched in 1957, that spurred passage of the National Defense Education Act and increased spending in science education in this country). Governor Reagan said to me, "Will you tell me how increasing the salaries of teachers who are running ineffective schools is going to help those schools?" I said, "I can't. There is no way this will do that." I added that it would be very difficult for him to veto the bill, "because everyone will tell you that to do so will be political suicide; that you'll never be reelected." He looked me in the eye and said, "Cap, I didn't come here to get reelected." That was a refreshing change.

When he came into office, he found a huge deficit, much bigger than anyone expected. (California, like most states, requires a balanced budget, but Reagan's predecessor, Pat Brown, had been paying twelve months' worth of bills with fifteen months' worth of revenue, through bookkeeping changes.) Reagan was persuaded that he simply had to raise taxes if we were to keep faith with the state constitution. It went against the grain, but he did it. By the end of his first year in office, 1967, it was apparent he had turned things around and that there would even be a small surplus the following spring. I wanted him to know about this first, because as soon as the legislature knew about it they would have all kinds of ideas of how to spend it. I told him I thought he should get a message out right away and asked him what he wanted to do about the surplus. "Why don't we just give it back?" he asked. I said, "Well, it's never been done before." "No," he replied, "but then you've never had an actor for governor before, either." So we gave it back.

His remarkable personality stands out. He was a happy man, secure and serene. He knew who he was and he didn't have to impress anybody or try to be somebody he wasn't. From time to time, people would ask me, "What's he *really* like?" My reply was always along these lines: He's exactly the way you see him. There is no difference between the public and private man. He is happy and he wants other people to be happy. He's delighted if he can leave you laughing. On the serious side, he has many good ideas and he knows what he wants to achieve. He's not going to be too rigid. He has a philosophical rudder, but he's never going to let that rudder drive him up on the rocks. He won't so much compromise as take as much as he can get of what he wants under the circumstances, then come back later and try to get more. He always knows just where he wants to go. And he doesn't determine that by taking polls.

These days there is a lot of what passes for conventional wisdom to the effect that Reagan really didn't do anything as President, beyond making people feel good. Indeed, he did make the American people feel good about themselves, and that's quite an accomplishment, because when people feel good about themselves they will be more productive and energetic. But he did a great deal more. A firm goal in his mind as he took office was that he wanted to make sure communism didn't expand any further and then to defeat it—without a war.

I recall in December 1980, during the transition before his inauguration, we began to get briefings about a lot of Soviet threats, including the possibility they might invade Poland. They had a couple of divisions on the Polish border and were reinforcing them with more troops. We were discussing this in a meeting. I told the President-elect that I thought he had to let them know as strongly as we could that any attempt to expand what they had in Poland would bring an immediate and aggressive response from the United States. "Well then, we'll tell them that," he said. Coming out of that meeting, I took him aside and told him that the United States wasn't in a position to actually *do* anything about the situation, other than send a strong message, because we simply did not have the military capacity. I told him I had received a briefing to the effect that the arms gap was even greater than we had thought when we were out on the campaign trail. He said, "Cap, we must never be in this position again. Right from the beginning we are going to regain that military strength." He repeated what he had said many times out on the stump: "If it ever came to a choice of balancing the budget or regaining our defense strength, there isn't any question in my mind what we must do." He intended to get that strength back so we could do something about Soviet aggression and could prevent them from fulfilling their agenda, which was domination of the world. He of course proceeded along those lines, in the face of a lot of criticism. Many people criticized him during those first two years because he was the only President not to get an arms control agreement. He said that didn't make any difference to him because the past arms control agreements only limited the rate of increase of arms. That wasn't what he wanted. He wanted arms reduction. And he got it. By October 1987, he got the first treaty not only to reduce arms, but also to eliminate an entire class of weapons. He knew what he wanted and his policy initiatives are what won the cold war.

The Strategic Defense Initiative—SDI—was a real part of it. The Soviets had been working on this almost from the moment they signed the ABM treaty. The treaty, in effect, banned any kind of defense against nuclear missiles. It was a terrible mistake for us to sign, but the Soviets weren't bothered by it because they simply paid no attention to it. The theory that was prevalent in those days was that you are only safe when you are vulnerable. Ronald Reagan never believed that. (We had even discussed it when he was governor.) He was determined to get an effective defense against those weapons. The Soviets had been working on just such a project. They knew we had the resources and talent to develop a successful defense. We just hadn't exhibited the political will to do it until Ronald Reagan came on the scene. His speech announcing the SDI in March 1983 supplied the missing ingredient.

It began to dawn on the Soviets that they couldn't possibly win such a race. It played itself out in Gorbachev's futile efforts to make communism more effective and open. The Soviet system soon collapsed.

The Clinton policy of attempting to gut the strategic defense program is a serious mistake. They have gone back to the old idea that the ABM, with its no-defense emphasis, is what we need. In fact, we should take the steps necessary to get out of the ABM treaty. President Reagan was the first to reject this notion that you are only completely safe if you are completely vulnerable. After his SDI speech, he was subjected to great scorn and derision, but he kept at it for the rest of his administration. We managed to make a great deal of progress in securing that kind of defense, and we can still have it. There is nothing impossible about it, at all.

KIRK WEST

PRESIDENT, CALIFORNIA CHAMBER
OF COMMERCE

"The reporters roared with laughter."

Kirk West has headed the California Chamber of Commerce since 1986. Before that, he served as secretary of business, transportation and housing in the administration of Governor George Deukmejian. During the Reagan years in Sacramento, he served as chief deputy state controller and deputy director of the Department of Finance.

Two things spring to mind: the way Governor Reagan prepared for his press conferences and the way he conducted his cabinet meetings. I sat in on these off and on for six of his eight years in Sacramento, first as the deputy finance director, then as chief deputy controller. In the first job, I represented the directors, first Cap Weinberger, then Verne Orr; in the second job, I represented Controller Houston Flournoy.

Reagan's senior staff would meet with him early every Tuesday morning before his weekly press conference. Cabinet officers would often attend. The group would brief him as to what the press corps was talking about. I recall that, at one point, Jesse Unruh and George Moscone, the respective State Assembly and Senate leaders—both Democrats—were carrying on a concerted and coordinated attack on Reagan. I don't recall the particular issue, only that they appeared to be very angry.

The press secretary and our people from the Department of Finance furnished the information to rebut what Unruh and Moscone were claiming, along the lines of, "They say this has increased by 14 percent when it's only gone up 8 percent"—that sort of thing. We had all the statistical refutations and Reagan absorbed them all.

Reagan went across the hall to the press conference room and the first question was, "What do you think of the charges of Senator Moscone and Assembly Speaker Unruh?" And, Reagan says, "Well, I thought George was at his best when he was terribly angry and Jesse was at his best when he was terribly hurt." The reporters roared with laughter. He knew how to make his rivals look like a couple of posturing politicians. He didn't give them credibility by indulging in a statistical tug-of-war. In fact, he didn't use a single statistic. He defused the entire issue with that one friendly jibe. It was amazing.

I remember well, also, the debate over the Dos Rios dam. It was 1968. The administration was divided. The water establishment, led by Bill Gianelli, head of Water Resources, and Earl Coke, secretary of agriculture, and several others, were pushing for this dam. It would have flooded Round Valley in Mendocino County. It was to be a federal dam and no project of that sort had ever been stopped before.

As the project moved along, "Ike" Livermore, secretary of resources (I was one of his assistants at the time, my first job in the Reagan administration), and Bill Mott, director of the Parks Department, were trying to stop it. It was all uphill for them.

The cabinet meetings were going on and on. One day, Ike was droning on about twenty or so reasons why the dam was a bad idea and he said, "Another point is, this would violate our treaties with Indians" (there were mainly Indian ranchers in Round Valley). Earl Coke broke in and said, "Now this is a silly argument." That was the wrong thing to say to Reagan. He slapped the table and said, "That's not silly. Those treaties are our word." He really made a big thing of it and everybody squirmed with embarrassment. That was years before sensitivity toward Indian concerns was politically popular.

Shortly after that, Reagan announced he was opposed to the Dos Rios project and called for a study of alternatives. That killed the dam for good.

Reagan really used the cabinet as a policy device. He had a very structured method. He'd frequently say, in closing debate on an issue, "We didn't come to Sacramento to do that." He knew what he wanted and he was very well organized.

Reagan relied on his cabinet a lot. I think no governor before or since had such a structured, well-organized procedure for decision making. There were a lot of subjects to be covered. We all had fun with the dictum "Put it on one page" (which the proponents had to do with every issue), but that method of summarizing an issue led to focused, healthy discussion of the issues.

CHARLES Z. WICK
DIRECTOR, UNITED STATES INFORMATION
AGENCY, 1981–88

"That's the way it's going to be, and I'm a stubborn bastard."

Until he became the longest-serving director in the history of the USIA, Charlie Wick was an independent businessman. His interests are wide. He earned his bachelor's degree in music at the University of Michigan, then earned a law degree at Case Western Reserve. In business, he is a venture capital and real estate investor. He served as cochairman of the first Reagan inaugural, in 1981. As director of the USIA, he oversaw the initiation of Worldnet, a satellite television service, Radio Marti, the Artistic Ambassador program, and other innovations.

Radio Marti, which has been broadcasting to the people of Cuba since 1985, has been a great success, but it almost didn't get launched. The idea for it came in the early days of the Reagan administration, but it wasn't until fall 1983 that Congress passed the Radio to Cuba Act. At the last minute, rather than setting up a new agency to run it, they told me it was going to be put under the USIA. I was asked how I felt about that and said, "Fine. We already have the Voice of America, so it's logical."

We had to put together an organization from scratch to manage and operate Radio Marti. We rented a vacant building near the USIA headquarters. We installed Radio Marti on four floors and started hiring people. I was determined to be very careful about our planning because Castro was incensed over the fact there would be such an undertaking. In fact, to warn and intimidate us, he was using two 500,000-watt transmitters to make a million-watt jamming operation that knocked several Florida radio stations off the air. By doing that, he had declared his intention to do whatever he could to hamper the Radio to Cuba Act. With this as background, I felt that rather than start modestly and expand the operating hours incrementally from an hour or two a day, it could make the maximum impact by going on the air full-time from the very first day. Our initial target was eighteen hours a day.

We added more people and began rehearsing with simulated broadcasting schedules. My goal was to go on the air May 20, 1985, which was the 150th anniversary of the birth of José Martí. He had created the only democracy Cuba had ever known. It was short-lived, but he was revered as a great patriot.

During that period, the two U.S. senators from Florida—Lawton Chiles, a Democrat, and Paula Hawkins, a Republican—came to see me. They were anxious to get Radio Marti on the air and thought I might be dragging my feet. I told them we were rehearsing and working out a plan to resist Castro's jamming. They were quite polite, but there was a slightly intimidating note in Chiles's voice to the effect that, if we were trying to string him along, there would be a lot of trouble for us. In fact, I had the backing of nearly all the Democrats as well as the Republicans in Congress. This was not a partisan effort.

The preparations went ahead in 1984 and into the early months of 1985. By April, I wanted to brief the National Security

Council to tell them we were ready to go. I tried to reach the President's national security adviser, John Poindexter. He gave me the brush-off. I couldn't get him on the phone. His assistant called back and said he could see me in a couple of months. I replied, "Just tell him that we are about ready to launch Radio Marti next week." That got his attention! He called right back and said, "You are not going on the air. It would be too dangerous." I said, "I am going on the air with Radio Marti unless the President tells me not to." Since we were under a congressional mandate, it would have been difficult to stop the project. That was a Thursday, as I recall. Poindexter immediately set up an NSC meeting for Friday.

There we were, meeting in the basement of the White House in the Situation Room, around the long table. Along with President Reagan were Chairman of the Joint Chiefs of Staff, General John Vesey; Secretary of State George Shultz; Defense Secretary Cap Weinberger; CIA Director Bill Casey, and others. The President opened the meeting and invited me to make my case. I gave the chronology of the project, discussed our people and their readiness, and pointed out that in the daytime 80 percent of the Cuban people on the western half of the island would be able to hear us and the other 20 percent could get us at night. I said we expected jamming and explained how I thought we could minimize it.

The President went around the room, asking each person to make comments. General Vesey said he was uncomfortable about timing (this was only a few days ahead of the Martí birthday anniversary). He talked about how Castro might jam us; we'd jam him and so on until we might be forced to drop a bomb on one of his transmitters and where would we go from there?

Others had similar reservations. One Cabinet officer said he didn't think we should be in a position where Castro might think we were now bluffing. President Reagan said, "I think Castro already thinks we are bluffing." He added, "Charlie, you go ahead. We're going to go on the air." He got up to leave for another meeting. As he opened the door, he said, "Now listen, everyone, I don't want any more good-faith arguments for a delay, because that's the way it's going to be and I'm a stubborn bastard!"

He said that with a smile, of course. His sense of humor has always been one of his great assets. He could use it to drive home a point, or just enjoy a good laugh. I recall a story he told at the 1987 summit with Gorbachev in Washington. I still have a photo of the farewell luncheon with Gorbachev's head thrown back in a great laugh. Reagan had just recounted a story I had told him the night before: It seems Gorbachev had put restrictions on the hours liquor could be sold so as to reduce alcoholism and drunk driving in the Soviet Union. It was a big campaign. So one July morning, following a weekend at his country dacha, he was a little late getting back to the Kremlin to attend to business. Since the police had been alerted to crack down on all speeders, he knew what would happen if they went too fast. So he said to his driver, "You better get in the backseat and let me drive." Then, sure enough, as the speeding limo approached the Kremlin, four police cars descended on it. The occupants of three of the police cars watched as the fourth one approached the limo. They saw him have a brief conversation with the driver, then back off as the limo sped away. When the policeman walked back to his colleagues, they said, "What's going on? Why didn't you arrest him?" He replied, "Oh, this guy is way too important to arrest." They reminded him of the crackdown on speeders. One of them said, "If this guy was so important, just who was he?" The other said, "I don't know who he was, but his driver was Gorbachev!"

Speaking of Gorbachev, the friendship that he and Reagan developed through the summit process has continued. Gorbachev was the first recipient of the Ronald Reagan Freedom Award, given at the Reagan Library in 1992. Gorbachev, his wife, and daughter all came. It was a happy and successful day. Here was a genial man who had headed an adversary nation—the "evil empire"—joking with Reagan and the rest of us. At one point, he turned to me and said, "Now that we're friends, maybe you can help us. You sure did cause us a lot of trouble with that Voice of America!"

Looking back to 1979, before the 1980 campaign for the presidency, my wife, Mary Jane, and I encouraged Ronnie to run. One night that spring, he was out giving a speech. We were having dinner with Nancy. Mary Jane and I said we'd like to hold a luncheon to raise some money for his campaign "exploratory" committee that had just been formed. My worry was that if some of the people we wanted to contribute couldn't attend, it would be much more time-consuming (and not as productive) to make a lot of individual calls. Nancy said she appreciated our willingness to help and hoped we'd find a way. Mary Jane and I talked it over. We knew the Reagan campaign exploratory committee was strapped for cash (they were operating out of an office near the Los Angeles airport) and that most of the cocktail receptions held to raise funds up to that point had raised relatively small amounts (in the $12,000 to $16,000 range). That's when we hit upon the idea of asking eleven couples who were good friends of ours to cosign Western Union Mailgrams collectively to all our friends, inviting them to join the "Ground Floor Committee." We said in the Mailgram that the first meeting would be held at our house on June 27, 1979, and that the second meeting would be held two years later at the White House.

We figured that if no one replied, we'd still have the contributions from each of the twelve couples (at $2,000 per couple). That would total more than their average fund-raiser. As it turned out, the response was great. The evening of his appearance at our house, we set up a platform on our patio so that everyone could see Ronnie when he gave his remarks (not being able to actually see the candidate is a common problem at fund-raisers held at homes). The response was electric. We wound up with $80,000 for the campaign and a boost of enthusiasm for the Reagan candidacy from his hometown!

After the event, I made up a manual, a checklist of all the things to remember in putting together such a fund-raising event. Several people asked me for copies and organized their own events. Shortly thereafter, in August, John Sears, the campaign director, and Mike Deaver, the deputy director, came to see me and asked if I would join the fund-raising effort full-time. I said I would think about it.

That summer we had taken a house at Trancas, on the ocean. The weekend the Reagans were coming out to visit us I had been thinking about the meeting with Sears and Deaver. The Reagans, Mary Jane, and I were strolling on the beach when I said, "You know, I have an idea. Why don't we arrange to have the dinner at which you announce your candidacy in New York? It's the media center of the country. It will surprise people, because no one thinks of it as 'Reagan country.' I'll at least help to get it started." The Reagans liked the idea. In early September, Mary Jane and I went to New York.

The first thing we needed to do was form a host committee. Bill Casey (later to head the CIA in the Reagan administration) invited us to lunch to discuss it. Max Raab, a prominent attorney who later was Reagan's ambassador to Italy, joined us. We decided that $500 a ticket was the right price. To encourage people who lived in Connecticut and New Jersey to come, we offered tickets for their kids at $35, the actual cost of the dinner.

I arranged with the New York Hilton Hotel to reserve part of their big ballroom (it could be divided with sliding panels). As the tickets were sold, we increased the size of our ballroom by increments until, by the time of the event, we had filled the entire room. About 1,850 people attended. That was in addition to 250 media people in the balcony. Our son, C.Z., and some friends had put together an excellent short film on Reagan and did it pro bono. At its finish, the room went dark and, stepping into the spotlight, was the candidate himself. He gave a great speech. Later that night, it was broadcast on a special television network we had put together. It got a tremendous amount of attention and the campaign was launched.

The Reagans and Mary Jane and I have been good friends for a long time and have shared a lot of happy times together. As I look over Ronald Reagan's years in the public limelight, I think the secret of his success is his enormous personal integrity, together with the incomparable support of his beloved Nancy.

PETE WILSON
THIRTY-SIXTH GOVERNOR OF CALIFORNIA

"Ronald Reagan thinks it may have been his best scene. I'm convinced of it."

Pete Wilson and Ronald Reagan first became acquainted following their first election to office in 1966—Reagan as California's governor and Wilson to the State Assembly. Wilson went on to become mayor of San Diego, where he served for more than a decade, then was twice elected to the United States Senate. He was elected governor of California in 1990 and reelected in 1994.

My favorite Ronald Reagan story was one he told me himself. It was his account of his private conversation with the Soviet leader, Mikhail Gorbachev, on the occasion of their first summit meeting in Geneva in November 1985.

Their formal talks were to be held in a palace on the heights overlooking the lake, but before the official sessions were to begin, the President wanted to have an informal chat with Gorbachev, with only their interpreters present. President Reagan chose a little-used boat house by the lake as the site for this chat. He directed that a fire be lit in the fireplace to take the seasonal chill off the old place.

The two men sat by the fire, at first making small talk and exchanging pleasantries. Then, President Reagan turned the conversation to talk of children. As he had hoped, it seemed to establish some common ground between them. After a time, he turned and stared thoughtfully at the fire. When he turned back to Gorbachev, Reagan looked directly into his eyes and—in what he later described to me as his "most plaintive, wistful tone"— said, "I do hope for the sake of our children that we can find some way to avert this terrible, escalating arms race . . ."

As Reagan paused, Gorbachev—thinking the President had completed his thought—smiled slyly, unable to mask a sudden look of triumph in his eyes. After several seconds, Gorbachev opened his mouth to respond, but before he could, Reagan continued, ". . . because, if we can't, America will not lose it, I assure you."

As he waited for the interpreter to translate his words into Russian, the President continued looking into Gorbachev's eyes—just as he was looking into mine when, years later, he told me this story. Gorbachev met his gaze, but the brief look of triumph had gone from his eyes. He nodded his understanding. After a few moments of silence, President Reagan, assuming the air of genial host, put a friendly hand on Gorbachev's shoulder and said, "Well, I've really enjoyed our conversation, but now I guess we had better get ready for dinner."

I'm sure the grin he gave Gorbachev at that moment was the easy, warm one he gave me as he told me the story. It was certainly the same grin he had given me when we met at the White House just before he left for Geneva. At that time, he held up a printed blue index card, put it into his inside coat pocket and, patting the pocket, said, "Wilson's Five Principles—got 'em right here."

I laughed, slightly embarrassed. In anticipation of the President's first summit with Gorbachev, liberal Democrats in and outside Congress had let loose a barrage of speeches, op-eds, and other public statements—all urging the President to make, in my opinion, dangerously misguided arms control concessions to Gorbachev. In response to this outpouring of bad advice, I had made a statement on the floor of the Senate urging entirely different counsel. I put forth five principles that I believed should guide U.S. arms control negotiations with the Soviets. Essentially, these urged a tough stance that could fairly—but simply—be characterized as "Don't give away the store!"

A patriotic organization dedicated to preserving strong defenses for the nation had given wide circulation to my speech and printed the negotiating principles it contained on blue index cards. It was one of those cards that President Reagan had put in his pocket.

I don't think Ronald Reagan needed that card—or anyone else's advice—any more than he needed a screenwriter or director for that scene he played with Gorbachev in the boat house by the lake. But I do wish there had been a camera and a sound crew on hand to record it for posterity, for I am convinced that it was that scene that set the stage—and, in fact, created the denouement—for the last act of the forty-year drama we called "The Cold War."

Of course, there were no cameras, no lights, no sound crew, to capture that scene and replay it to a worldwide audience. There were only four people present at that moment of quiet exchange in the late afternoon chill of a November day: the two principal actors on the world stage and their interpreters. But, Ronald Reagan's performance was compelling to the only audience that mattered. He believed what he said in that simple, unforgettable line declaring unequivocally that America would not lose the arms race. Ronald Reagan believed it, and so did Mikhail Gorbachev. And, as they say, the rest is history.

Ronald Reagan thinks it may have been his best scene. I'm convinced of it.

RICHARD B. WIRTHLIN
PRESIDENTIAL POLLSTER

"Dick, I know what we can do. I'll just have to go out and get shot again."

Richard Wirthlin's career began in academia. After earning his doctorate at the University of California (Berkeley), he taught economics and statistics there, at the UC Medical School, and at Brigham Young University. In 1969, he founded the Wirthlin Group, a strategic opinion research group that he heads to this day. He was Ronald Reagan's pollster and a trusted analyst and adviser, from the governorship through the presidency.

When I first met Ronald Reagan, he was in his first term as governor of California. In my view at that time, he was an actor playing out of his league and dabbling in politics, fired only by right-wing dogma. I would not have considered working for him. But the peculiar circumstance of our first meeting led me down an unexpected path, one that eventually resulted in my having the President of the United States as a client.

It began in late 1968, when I received a telephone call from a John Green in New York. Green asked if I would do a study for a group of Republicans interested in issues of concern to the California electorate. I agreed, and when it was finished I met Green at a Los Angeles hotel. As I began to explain how my data would be presented to a large group, Green interrupted. He said his name was not Green but Tom Reed, a well-known California Republican figure.

He went on to say that I would not be presenting the information to a group, but to an audience of one: Governor Reagan. I was surprised and somewhat aghast. Reed told me he had used this ruse because he was concerned that if I knew the identity of my audience in advance I might have turned down the assignment. A good friend of mine had helped Reagan in his 1966 gubernatorial campaign and I had chided him for "selling out" to a Hollywood actor. Now, it seemed, I was in my friend's shoes.

Reed and I rode in silence to Governor Reagan's home in Pacific Palisades. There, the governor ushered me into his small library, where we spent the next two hours going over my data and analysis. I was impressed with his intelligence, sensitivity, and his uncanny ability to go right to the heart of a complex issue. I found that his opinion of America's promise and his innate optimism paralleled my own. Thus, my preconceptions of a heavy-handed, right-wing actor-turned-politician were blown away. I decided I had just met a man with more raw leadership ability than I had known. That is how it began.

Over the years, that ritual of my bringing Ronald Reagan data and discussing its political and policy implications was to be repeated many times and in many places.

One of the most difficult presentations I ever made to him occurred on an airplane. On the Monday before the 1976 New Hampshire primary, I joined the campaign tour in Illinois. That night, aboard our chartered jet, John Sears, the campaign manager, asked me to tell Reagan how difficult the situation had become in New Hampshire. After the plane took off, I moved into the seat next to Reagan and gave him a review of the situation. "It's going to be extremely close, Governor, and it looks to me like we could well lose it," I concluded. For a few moments, he was quiet. He looked out the window just as the lights of Manchester, New Hampshire, came into view. Finally, he said, "Well, Dick, I do hope someone down there will light a candle for me tonight." Alas, any candles lit that night did not translate into enough votes to give Reagan a win in New Hampshire.

The best news I ever took to Reagan was also delivered on an airplane. In 1980, he had decided to finish his campaign in San Diego. While there, I learned he would win by a landslide the next day. Back on the plane, Nancy Reagan turned to me and asked, "Dick, what is going to happen tomorrow?" I told my news. Reagan was somewhat superstitious, however, and did not believe that "the game is over until it's really over." So the real celebration did not occur until the next day. But I knew from the way the Reagans responded that they realized they were going to have to start planning the packing of their belongings for the move to Washington, D.C.

Over the years, I took to the President a full share of disappointing news. I recall a wet, cold, overcast afternoon in January 1983. I had just learned that half of all Americans disapproved of the way President Reagan was handling his job. When I was ushered into the Oval Office, I came right to the point. I told him that for the first time since he had taken office, a majority disapproved of his job performance. The news sobered him at first. Then, as I watched him, I noticed a twinkle in his eye. He said, "Dick, I know what we can do. I'll just have to go out and get shot again." We both laughed. Then he added, "Don't worry about it, Dick. Everything is going to turn out just fine."

And of course, it did.

INDEX

PHOTOGRAPHS
